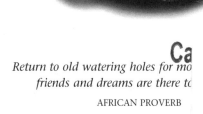

Ca
Return to old watering holes for mo
friends and dreams are there to
AFRICAN PROVERB

D1323933

Old Watering Holes

Mayo to Serabu

Hilary Lyons

DUDU NSOMBA PUBLICATIONS

GLASGOW

First published 2001 by

DUDU NSOMBA PUBLICATIONS
4 Gailes Park,
Bothwell,
Glasgow,
Scotland
Telephone : 01698854290
Fax: 01698854472

Cover by Steven Hope

ISBN : D-9522233-8-4

Designed and typeset by
Steven Hope Design

Printed and bound by
Ardmore Press,
35 Ardmore Park,
Artane
Dublin 5

Dedication

To the memory of my parents Bridget and Richard Lyons
who gave me my first sense of the presence of God all
around us; to Bishop Shanahan and the Dominican
Mothers whose inspiring vision was passed on to me; to the
people of Sierra Leone who accepted me and to
Sir Milton Margai, the first Prime Minister of Independent
Sierra Leone who guided my first steps in the country.

Acknowledgements

I have to thank Leah Atwater of Ann Arbor, Michigan for her energy and determination in making me write these stories in the first place when we met in Sierra Leone.

Thanks to the well-known author Angeline Kelly who helped me with grammar and content; Dr. Rosemary McMahon who worked with me in Sierra Leone, and gave valuable help on health and medical content; Helen Wynne who put me through my grammar paces in a final editing.

Sister Elizabeth Onwuama, Nigerian Holy Rosary Sister and Rev. Sahr Yambasu, a Sierra Leonean, Circuit Minister of the Methodist Church, Arklow, gave helpful advice from an African perspective.

Many thanks to Sisters Monica Devine, Franca Onyibor, Edith Dynan, Bride Darcy, Miriam Tracy, Anne Coleman, Catherine Halley, Breda Hession, Celia Doyle, Mary Coleman and a host of others who made suggestions, proof read and gave constant support. I must also mention the sisters who kept the project alive by asking: "When is the book coming out?" Thank you.

Friends like Kathleen Speprduto and Annie Doyle waded through early versions and gave invaluable advice.

A very sincere thank you to my country man from Louisburgh, Rev. Pádraig Ó Máille SPS who not only did initial editing but when he saw my energies flagging put his shoulder to the wheel and got the wagon rolling.

My dear friend Susan Bloom provided the funds that made the book possible and has my lasting gratitude.

Foreword

This book began the day Leah Atwater said to me: "don't *tell* me another story, write them and I will type them" and so she did. Selecting some of them to share among family and friends has been more difficult.

The stories are memories from home and from Serabu, Sierra Leone where I spent over forty years. Some memories are sad but not all. Sierra Leone was not a sad country.

The last chapter deals, briefly, with the anarchic war that has ravaged Sierra Leone for over ten years. The war has received extensive media coverage which, sadly, has obscured the reality of this quiet and beautiful country; a country of mainly rural farmers much like farming people anywhere.

During the fighting all our hospital buildings were destroyed. For me and for many others this was a real heartbreak. But how much more so for the people of Serabu, who are left grieving for many of their loved ones.

I have tried to have the historical facts correct, perception of events and encounters is mine. Liberties have been taken with the Krio language to make it more comprehensive for readers in English. Names of patients and some villages have been changed.

The title is taken from an African proverb which says: "Return to old watering holes for more than water– friends and dreams are there to meet you." At these memory wells I have been refreshed though sometimes the water contained the salt of tears, tears that cleanse and heal.

Contents

1

The Colony

The townland where I was born and grew up is called The Colony and is situated about five miles west of the town of Louisburgh in County Mayo. Louisburgh sits on the extreme South Western tip of Clew Bay, of which William Makepeace Thackeray wrote: "Clew Bay is a miracle of beauty. It forms an event in one's life to have seen that place so beautiful is it, and so unlike all other beauties that I know of."

The name of the townland dates back to the time of the famine. In 1845 the potato crop – the staple food – failed, and ushered in one of the great famines of history. Disadvantaged areas like the West, where the crop was coaxed out of rock-ridden fields at the best of times, were the worst affected. Ridges where the potatoes rotted were never dug out and can be seen on the hillsides to this day. The population was decimated, many died, those who could emigrate did so, mainly to the United States and England.

A group calling itself the 'Society for the Protection of Conscience' set up relief stations called 'Colonies'. There was one on Achill Island also. They were proselytising Protestant groups and it is alleged and fairly well documented, that accepting the Protestant faith was a criterion for receiving supplies. The food offered was called 'soup' and contemptuously referred to thereafter as 'the soup'. 'Taking the soup' left a very bad mark on the family escutcheon and is still remembered. Those who accepted Protestantism were called 'jumpers', probably an anglicisation of the Irish verb 'to turn', 'iompaigh'.

A community centre, a school, a church and staff houses were established. The whole area belonged to Lord Sligo and when the redistribution of land came about as a result of the efforts of the Land League, my grandfather bought the steward's house and land where we lived. Right beside it was the Protestant church and a small cemetery. At this stage I can just remember it. The church is now a grassy mound.

Eventually the Protestant families died out and there are none there any more. In passing it should be mentioned that the Catholic Church, not to be outdone in what we would now call fundamentalism, excommunicated the 'jumpers' for apostasy. Re-admission to the Catholic Church was by special ceremony. It was said that the poor people, frightened for their immortal souls, crowded to preached 'missions' and would pass the only top coat they had from one to the other before presenting themselves for confession to the 'Missioner'. Fear of an avenging God was prevalent.

Coming nearer to the year of my birth the times were straitened. The rebellion of 1916 (the year my parents married) was followed by a Civil War, which ceased in 1922. There was a new government, a new constitution and an empty treasury. The Colony holding was 180 acres of which 80 were bog; the remainder needed draining and reclaiming.

How my parents, especially my father, who was not young at the time, hoped to raise and educate a large family and protect them from the anxiety that must have walked with them is not clear. And yet they did, and lived to eighty-two and ninety-two years old respectively, without stress, illness, or incapacity. They were, like everybody in the area, deeply religious, almost to the point of superstition. If God gave life, he would sustain it. Contraception was undreamed of. Hard manual work was the norm. Virtues they believed in were caring and providing for their children, and being truthful and honest in their dealings with others, generous, and hospitable. My father in particular was referred to as a 'dacent' man, which meant, among other things, not taking a mean advantage, paying one's debts – and going to everyone's funeral.

My mother was fiercely proud and possessive; my father, gentler, was head of household only in name. She, like many Irish mothers, ruled the roost. She demanded, and got, obedience. You were good if you did what you were told. If you were good, God was pleased and you would go to Heaven when you died. If you were bad, she redressed the situation with a few swipes on the bottom with a thin sally rod from the garden.

She was also light-hearted and fun loving. On Sunday evenings I can remember sitting with her and father on Sheeaun Hill and rolling down to the bottom. All the fields had Irish names: Garrai Dhiarmuid (Dermot's Garden), Sean Bhaile (Old Town), Pairc an Asail (Donkey's Field), Teanga (Tongue – a sliver of a field aptly named). In a nearby farm is Leaba Dhiarmuda (Dermot's bed). Did Diarmuid and Gráinne pass this way in their flight from Fionn? It is said that the pursuit was so hot, that the lovers only spent one night anywhere. This may account for the many 'Leabaigh' to be found in different parts of Ireland. The mythology of ancient Ireland was eerily close and created in us a great sense of mystery and magic – and belonging.

Childhood: Life was hard in the country in the nineteen twenty's and thirty's. There were nine of us. The winters were long, cold and wet. There was no indoor plumbing or electricity. The tractor had not yet come to alleviate the heavy physical demands made by the plough, scythe, spade and shovel on the men-folk. Travel was by sidecar or on foot in all weathers. It was the norm for children to make their contribution to the work both on the farm and in the house as soon as they were able. It was not so idyllic to be sent out for a can of water or a 'brehsin' of turf on a bitterly cold winter's evening or night; nor was it nice to have to milk the small black cow whose milk came reluctantly from her teats, making the exercise a prolonged one. The small black cow could also tire of the exercise and whack you with her tail or, worse still, raise her hind leg and with a sharp well-aimed kick send the milk flying across the shed. There was no sweet shop around the corner and no cinema down the street. I saw my first film at thirteen years of age.

In spite of that life had its joys and excitements. I loved spring for its surge of new growth, the re-appearance of snowdrops, the dancing daffodils and the lengthening of the days. I remember when I was big enough (or small enough!) to look a wild iris – seileastrom – in the eye. Later in the year there would be meadow sweet, foxglove, loosestrife, forests of montbresia and fuscia dripping blood red in the setting sun.

There were calves, lambs and chickens to be fed and loved. Summer, which seemed to be always fine, was a mixture of chores and delights. Taking the cows home through the river for milking, long evenings spent at the beach or at the clapper bridge made, in memory at least, for halcyon summers.

Of all the magic places that were safe for small children in summer was the Clapper Bridge, situated about five hundred yards from our home. This consisted of some thirty stone pillars about three feet high and one yard apart. A large flat stone was laid across between the pillars. These were loose and clapped when you walked over them. That may be the reason it was called the 'clapper'. It was built around the time of the Society for Relief (1845 or thereabouts), supposedly to make for easier access to the 'soup'. Whatever about the name it was a place of enchantment for us children. Two streams met there, one from Feenone and one from Cloonlara. We waded there, we brought the cows home through the stream in the evening, we looked for eels and oysters, we hid under the bridges, created small lakes and dams, we lay flat on the stones gazing contemplatively for hours on end at "rose-moles all in stipple upon trout that swim", for the brown trout were at home there. You could catch one with your hand if you approached very, very slowly till you neared the unsuspecting prey swishing his tail and enjoying the sun, then slip fingers and thumb, with lightening speed, beneath the gills. Up either stream where the pools were deeper you could come on a salmon. Once, the whole family chased a salmon up and down the shallows till, exhausted, the fish surrendered. It would be difficult to assess the impact of that meeting of the waters at the ·Clapper Bridge on our lives in terms of our formation. I remember it teeming with life. Now when I sit there an occasional 'pinkeen' rises for a fly but nothing like the myriad of living things that turned summer days to magic.

When we visited Aunt Mary in Leenane, she lost no opportunity to draw us into her own love for the scenery. She dreaded the summer storms and would sit huddled in the kitchen saying rosaries while they lasted. Then she would rise up and say: "Children! Sunset at the mouth of the Killary will be wonderful this evening."

And off we would go. Sure enough these were scenes never to be forgotten. The bay, tired from turbulence, now serenely reflected an untroubled sky and the mountains lay etched at the water's edge like a still water-colour. Streams foamed lustrously down the mountainsides to kiss the sleeping bay. A lazily setting sun played games with scattered clouds, tinting the hills, green, blue, and amethyst. We gazed in awe.

As we wound our way back past the hotel where the Guinness family were dining and wining their friends in, what seemed to us, great splendour, we longed to watch the other wonder of the world – shining silver ware, sparkling crystal, tall serviettes, ladies in evening gowns, but Aunt Mary would admonish: "Well brought up children never stare. Walk right on please!"

Like most people I have one special memory. On a visit to Leenane while staying at Killary Cottage with Aunt Sarah, my cousin Mary and I went each day from the house, crossed the road and stile to where the rocks sloped down to the water's edge. Special flowers grew there. As the tide receded small pools were left in the rock formation. For some reason, or for no reason at all, we spent the morning scooping water from these pools into bottles, using oyster shells. Called to lunch we ate heartily and galloped back to the warm rocks, the pretty flowers, the oyster shells, the trees nearby and the water mirroring back our faces. Did that occupation last an hour, a day, or several? I have no idea. That time, in whatever its measurement, remains locked in my treasure chest of memories, as a time when I was, for a space, completely happy, when, as it were, my being had no boundaries but fused with all around me.

Many years later, Mary was to ask me whether by any chance I too remembered those moments? It transpired that we both shared a moment of total peace when, for a time, Eternity enwombed two small girls draining rock pools with oyster shells.

School: After the thrills and excitements of childhood Mary Gibbons, or as she was called 'Mary Davy John', now Mrs O'Toole, took me by the hand and we set out for Killadoon National School, in September 1930. We crossed James Needham's field, the Burke's fields, and took the road as far as Mickey Lyons's, where we once more took to the fields and crossed the shoulder of the hill that stretches from Ailmore to Killadoon. It was about two miles. I wore, and was to wear for a few years to my bitterness, special boots, laced up at the sides and reaching almost to my knees. This was to protect my foot where, at the age of four, I had an osteomyelytis and spent three months in Castlebar Hospital. I hated those boots! In June, or May if it was fine, my peers took off their shoes and went barefoot to school. This was called 'going in our feet'. But not me. They paddled, dangled their feet in running streams, felt the delicious ooze of mud between their toes, but not me. They had hooks on the side, those boots, and Saylya had a pair like them. Celia, or Saylya as she was called, was an old lady who used to take care of us sometimes. She was very strict and had a gutsy repertoire of Irish curses, which she used with great abandon on occasion. "T'anam'n diabhal", she would yell at one of us, which meant something like 'your soul to the devil'. The four letter words in English had not yet arrived, or at least Saylya did not know them.

Having led me into the infant's class, Mary, who was a year or two older, went to the next classroom. After break, the boys came bounding in to tell us that two old brothers who lived close by were fighting. Those micro sadists embellished the scene. "Blood", they said, "is running down the road!" "They are killing each other!" "Sticks and stones!" The two men in question lived unattended in a shack near the school. From time to time they fought pitched battles, or so it was said. They were fearful to look at, having long hair, long beards and ragged clothes. I usually scampered past their house as if the devil was on my heels.

My first day at school on my own; no one to turn to! My small heart fluttered alternately from my mouth to the infamous boots. It is the first real fear I can remember and it marked me for life. To this day conflict, physical or psychological, paralyses me. Over the years I have twice intervened in fistfights, looking brave, but inside hoping no one could hear my knees knocking.

I remember Mrs Maguire introducing us to the Penny Catechism, for that was its price. It was a very small booklet and she would place it on her knee, script towards the scholar, and shoot the questions. If the emerging Christian failed to answer correctly by rote he or she got some small punishment such as staying late to learn the missed answers. Little of significance on the academic side stands out in my mind. A reasonable scholar, my progression from class to class went without problem.

At that time my brother Josie and I were developing what we imagined to be a sense of retributive justice. Our target was the small black cow that had horns and an unreasoning dislike for the old red cow. She would attack her unprovoked and we watched carefully when bringing home the cows for milking. One evening she got there before us and really hurt the old cow. We got a small thin rod and diverted her attention to her own rear, explaining to her at each stroke that she was young and she had horns and with that equipment it was not fair to attack the weak. Another evening I had an encounter with the gander. I had placed a basin of oats in their house for the ducks, only to find the geese had usurped the place and were eating the oats. I marched in to restore the rights of the ducks – smaller birds. The gander, hissing fiercely, neck outstretched and coming in low, got his teeth on my indignant pointing finger, held on and proceeded to lash me around the legs with his powerful wings. My screams brought my father and a better arrangement was made.

In summer we brought tea to the men saving the hay, breathing in the unforgettable sweet, fresh fragrance of new mown hay. We also brought tea to the bog when they were cutting or footing the turf. Saving the hay and the turf depended so much on the weather that everyone had to help or lose both crops. In winter there would frequently be cold, driving rain. The school 'central heating' consisted of a few sods of dismal smoking turf in the fireplace. There were no raincoats or other protective gear. We steamed away until we dried out. It is not true to say that we suffered no ill effects. Tuberculosis, meningitis and pneumonia were common.

Colony Liturgies: We had a Christmas Eve that no one else seems to have had. During Advent we said lots of extra Hail Marys to prepare for the coming of the Lord. That he would come gave us no problem; that Mary and Joseph might be looking for lodging was a real possibility; and anyhow, to show how we would welcome the Light of the World, two candles were lit in every window. Every house in the neighbourhood was similarly lit up, those on the hillsides looking especially beautiful. We would run up to the garden gate to admire them.

All day was spent cleaning and, though so near the winter solstice, it seemed to be the longest day in the year. We hopped about pestiferously asking mother: "Is it time to light the candles?" All windows had lace curtains. Miraculously we never set them on fire. The table would be prepared in the parlour for supper. This was a room reserved for visitors and special occasions. What today would be called the living room, was then called the kitchen. The kitchen had an open fireplace, a dresser, a dining table, and half a dozen or so straight backed chairs. It also had a 'settle-bed.' This was a wooden folding bed that served as a seat during the day and opened out to provide a bed at night. There was a large feather mattress inside and as it was situated in the room where the fire was, it was a very cosy place to sleep. With all the activities in that one room and many children, it was understandable that visitors were not normally admitted there. So the average comfortable house had a parlour. This doubled for a dining room and sitting room and was kept trim and tidy, for visitors. On special occasions, like Christmas, the family dined there. 'Tea in the room' was always a special occasion.

The fact that Christmas Eve was a fast day at that time seems to have escaped us completely. On that night the table was laden with all the good food we could provide, the centre-piece of the table being the beautiful iced cake that Mrs Butler sent from Dublin every year. The Butlers were rich relatives of mother's.

Even the Santa Claus mode was different. While other people hung their stockings on the end of the bed, we did not hang stockings at all but expected Santa to send whatever he was bringing, down the chimney on Christmas Eve, while we were all around. There were four possible fireplaces where this could happen so, having cleaned these thoroughly during the day, when evening came we kept checking these places excitedly. Mother would finally order us to our supper. During the meal she would announce that she was going to take a look at the candles. My Father would make sure that we stayed at table, thus giving her enough of time to put the parcels, which she had secreted in a convenient place during the day, in the fireplace. The first to spot a parcel would cry out: "He has come!" The sense of awe, the palpable evidence of the extra-terrestrial, on seeing something there, that was not there a moment ago, was fantastic. It passed and was followed by the opening of parcels, packages, shaking and shouting. Any packages and presents were wonder-full then. They bore no relation at all to today's toys in cost or sophistication.

At about 9 o'clock we would all, except my father and the very small ones, proceed over the clapper bridge to our nearest neighbour, Mrs. Prendergast, who was always called by her maiden name, Kate Needham. She was a gentle, friendly soul. We had sweet drinks and some more cake, then home again, pausing on the clapper bridge to watch the water and have a look at the stars. Which one guided the Wise Men?

Back home we waited till the stroke of midnight, when all the family knelt, with bare knees, on a cement floor (the latter was obligatory for some reason) and said three Hail Marys and so to bed. There must have been Christmas nights when the weather was bad, but I suppose we only went to Kate's on good nights. Anyway, I'm left with memories of crisp, starry or moonlit nights. It was later in life, I realised how many sacrifices my parents made, to give us those memories.

May is the month of Mary. That was a caption at school and it was often used as a headline for hand writing practice. In The Colony we prepared for her to visit us on May 1st. The day before, we would gather 'May flowers', correctly called primroses, in large quantities, and early on the first we scattered them at gateways and doorways for her feet to pass.

The ancient Celts had all sorts of rituals for the first of May, the purpose of which was, that there would be a good harvest for the coming year. It is nice to think that the Druids of Celtic Ireland cast their long shadows before them, infiltrating Christian thought to meet Mary – and dispel fear.

Easter! We were told that the sun dances with joy on Easter morning to celebrate Christ's rising from the tomb. There was no trouble about believing that, the miracle was to see the sun at all, on a cloudy morning in our misty Island. When we did see it, we looked and we looked and, at least to my own satisfaction, I once saw three gyrating orbs within the sun on one glorious spring morning. Maybe I stared too long. I knew nothing then about my Celtic ancestors who were sun worshippers and that their goddesses, Erin, Fola and Banba, made gracious precursors of the Father, Son and Spirit of the Christian Faith.

Saint Patrick's day in Mid-March was often very cold. Nonetheless we went out to gather the three leafed shamrock, packing it into our small red-cold hands and rushing in to mother, to ask if we had now collected enough. As often as not, she would detect a lot of clover, which had four leaves and once more the inexplicable would be explained, that there are only three Persons in One God, and we should go out and try again. This injunction might be softened by a large, long, slice of brown bread and butter, to sustain us as we searched for the real thing. We knew too, as does everyone in the whole, wide world, that Shamrock grows only in Ireland!

It was those small family liturgies that gave me my sense of an all-present, enveloping God, which is much more than I can say for the Penny Catechism or any of the Catechisms that followed.

2

Growing Up

Religion in childhood was a happy experience. The great beauty and myth of the environment made it easy for us "to turn but a stone and start a wing". Even though the God we learned from the Penny Catechism was a calculating sort of God, who rewards the good and punishes the wicked, we held it lightly. Sin, we were told, was divided into two categories, venial and mortal. If you died with venial sin on your soul, you would go to Purgatory. Purgatory was described in the Penny Catechism as a "place or state where some souls suffer for a time before they go to Heaven". If you died with mortal sin on your soul, you went to Hell for a-a-all Eternity. Not even God could do anything about that. We learned the Ten Commandments by heart and had first confession and first communion. Happy times except, that at seven years old, sin was not easy to comprehend. I confessed what ever my parents and teachers said was sinful such as: 'not saying my prayers', 'telling lies', and 'disobedience'. I did not feel bad.

Adolescence was a time of newness. In childhood new and fascinating discoveries were all around us; now they were within us.

A new awareness of self, who am I today, who will I be tomorrow; young men are interested in me, and I in them. At school my friends and I discussed our expectations of the ideal husband. He would be handsome, faithful, strong and gentle. We believed we would know him at first sight.

Dreams of love, romance and marriage we may have had, but there was a shadowy side to our dreams. We were not – absolutely not – to become pregnant outside of marriage. If we did, mortal sin with its 'Hell for all Eternity' got called on board, and created the fear that would keep us from this disaster. If it happened, hell began right away, for the poor girl would be thrust out of family and society never to return, with a ruthlessness that is difficult to relate to the Gospel of Jesus. Such women usually took refuge in convents specially set up for this 'charity' and remained there for the rest of their lives. Their babies were put up for adoption. There does not seem to have been any punishment for the man in the picture.

For something believed to be so menacingly serious the wonder remains, that we received virtually no formal education on the subject. We were warned, and watched, which was not very nice. The priests who came to preach Missions were stringent on sexual morality, as if this were the only commandment given to us. On the doorstep going to a dance, mothers or aunts would say: "now let ye be careful". We knew what they meant. But how did it come about that offences against this one commandment loomed so disproportionately large in our moral value system? No one ever warned us about any of the other commandments, like lies or dishonesty. This one does, of course, pack a bigger drive, a sort of street car that could take off on its own, wrecking family respectability, perceived norms of morality, not to mention the small life involved in an unplanned or unwanted pregnancy.

Being unlettered in this area meant that much of the normal erotica and sexual fantasies of our age were bunched together as 'bad thoughts' because we did not know what else to call them. So as such we mentioned them in Confession to be on the safe side. Confession I found to be an anxious and frustrating exercise. It played a large part in my life – and me not in the least bit sexually or sinfully daring. All good girls went once a week. Even later in the convent confessing such things as 'distraction at prayer', 'omitting prayers', 'speaking in anger', and maybe a sprinkling of 'bad thoughts' was futile because they would recur next week for sure. One sister complained to the priest that she was confessing the same thing every week only to be told she was lucky not to be breaking new ground every week.

If confession was a dreary excise for the penitent I dare not think what it must have been for the priest. "Hearing nun's confessions is like being nibbled to death by tame ducks" is attributed, rightly or wrongly, to Fr. Vincent McNabb. There was a priest who used to come for confession in the convent where over one hundred nuns filed in weekly for this exercise. He hated it. It was well known. He was in a country parish in County Cavan. It was in the 1940's, where mothers of large families with horrific workloads rode their bicycle, if they had one, or walked the miles it took to go to confession in Irish weather. So when a London-born novice began her confession softly with: "I came to confession a week ago" he interrupted with: "Ya hadn't faar ta come!" She rejoined us in chapel, her face red with suppressed laughter.

Years later, in Sierra Leone, I was to learn a lot more about the exercise of confession and reconciliation and their place in sustaining human relationships. There, confession is often to the person offended in presence of relevant members of the community. There are rituals of cleansing for some infringements of the moral code before the penitent is once more restored to harmony in the community.

Makes you think- Africa does.

St. Louis Convent: When I was thirteen years old, I was sent to St. Louis Convent, Balla, Co. Mayo. It was run by The Sisters of St. Louis who formed young women through a liberal education, sound discipline, good examination results and a strong faith in the value of the revival of our native Irish language.

Those who lived near attended on a daily basis– those who lived further away were accommodated as boarders. That meant full residential facilities for the three terms of the academic year. Being boarders meant, that as well as getting a good training, we were kept safe.

There were aspects of boarding school I hated. I hated the feeling of incarceration. There was no permission to go out to the town. Our letters, in and out, were opened. We went for long walks on Sundays, two by two, in a long, dreary formation with two nuns bringing up the rear. We wore navy gym frocks, blue jumpers, blazers, and black stockings. I detested black stockings.

I could not play the piano no matter how hard I tried nor could I, except with pain, do any form of mathematics. English and History I loved. When the English teacher came to class one day and while waiting for us to open our books, looked dreamily out the window and murmured:

"But look, the morn in russet mantle clad

Walks oe'r the dew of yon high Eastern hill", I knew I wanted to taste English like that. But a gift I discovered I had which gained me no credits was that of mimicry. I found I could imitate all the nuns, how they talked, walked, used their hands, and how their faces showed different moods. I became an entertainer. At study time, or in the dormitory, I could be found having everyone in 'stitches'. The Sisters thought my parents had better expectations of me than that and I received my one and only negative report. My parents were not pleased.

I imagined then that maybe I could become an actress or a writer, but felt called to mission and put those possibilities on hold. In the event I became neither, but a sense of humour and the love of a good book have been useful companions.

But that was that time and it was war-time. We heard news of the war on the wireless and we danced to Vera Lynn's 'We'll Meet Again', and 'Blue Birds over the White Cliffs of Dover', with remarkable insensitivity to the sadness enshrined in the lyrics, which can draw tears today.

Forced Landing at Emlagh: One great, war-related excitement we did have. In September 1942 I was visiting my aunt in Accony, when, in the early morning, we heard a plane roar over. This was not unusual and we always looked for identifying colours or logo. We watched especially for the Swastika. Someone shouted: "It's going to land!" and I was out of the house like a shot. Everyone else was outside their own doors staring skyward as a dark grey, medium sized, twin engine plane, barely missing the hedges at Emlagh, soared up over the hills, turned and came back, and disappeared from our view, clearly having landed.

Every man, woman and child, who had anything that went faster than feet, jumped upon it and made for Emlagh Point. Those who had only their legs used them. I had a bike and was there amongst the first. Emlagh Point is at the extreme south western tip of Clew Bay, looking out at New York, if Clare Island and Inis Turk did not block the view. A stretch of greensward called the Duach lies on the landside of the shoreline, stretching long enough to make a landing strip. There was a pervading fear of a German landing. To prevent the possibility of such an event, a local defence force had been established, as well as a coast guard force. These gentlemen were differently and impressively uniformed and had assembled small pyramids of round stones, at various points along the Duach, to prevent enemy landing. Though a relatively primitive defence mechanism, it made aircraft landing hazardous. The successful belly landing of this plane, by avoiding the stones without going on fire, was a miracle of piloting skill. A crowd of the concerned and the curious had gathered. Three young men alighted from the plane looking none the worse for their experience. They were Canadians, they said, and had run out of gas. Everyone tried to see and hear them, moving left, right, under elbows, over shoulders, the crowd, waving back and forth bursting with curiosity. Eventually the local defence representative presented himself to them. "Are you the local constabulary?" they asked. The gentleman in question claimed that honour and why wouldn't he? Would such a mighty event ever come his way again? In the meantime the coast guards arrived making the same claim, thereby confusing our guests, who up to now were not quite sure what country they were in. Eventually, the sergeant of the Guards cycled his way through the crowd to what now had become the biggest show ever. I don't know what passed at that official level but when we pressed them for information, as to where they took off from and where they were bound for, they were non-committal.

The Guards alerted the army and that evening truck loads of military came from Kildare. To add to all the excitement of real life drama, one of the trucks took the turn from the Accony road too close and the truck went into the ditch. Soldiers spilled out and jumped clear. No one was hurt unless military pride took a beating. The crew was taken to Kildare, the plane dismantled and removed. Only speculation remained. Who were they? What was their mission? Deserters? What could anyone want in Emlagh? Were they really short of gas? We were unable to find out, and were left wondering why three young Canadians, flying their country's colours, made a spectacular landing by a windy beach in the West of Ireland in 1942.

Or so it was until 1996 when the navigator of the plane, Mr Gill Drake decided to revisit the scene. His story: They took off from Gandor in New foundland in a plane called the Lockhead Ventura 460. It had a poor design and as a result a bad history. They were bound for Scotland but only half of the planes that set off with them ever arrived. For some time before the landing they knew the fuel supplies were exhausted and they would have to land, but where were they? They could see rugged territory. Could it be Scotland? Having touched down and alighted they asked eagerly: "Where are we?" "In Pat Joe McHale's duach!" That illuminating geographical location was eventually explained. The crew was taken to Belfast. They flew again and so did the plane, which had only its propellers damaged. The three young men survived the war.

3

Killeshandra

Ijoined the Missionary Sisters of the Holy Rosary at Killeshandra, Co. Cavan on the first of February 1943, six days before my 19th birthday. Bishop Joseph Shanahan C.S.Sp. had founded the congregation in 1924. Joseph Shanahan received his secondary and seminary education in France and on his return to Kimmage in 1902 was posted to the Nigerian Mission. There he was named Prefect Apostolic in 1905. Early in his missionary career he realised the value of education as a means of establishing the church. French Holy Ghost priests had staffed the Nigerian Mission up to that time. Education was not high on their agenda for a number of reasons: there was the language problem – English had become the official language under British influence; they were not trained teachers; their perception of spreading the Good News was limited to the care of orphans and the liberating of slaves. Shanahan disagreed with this, feeling that a church founded on slaves and orphans would have very little appeal to the Igbo people. He invited priests from the Irish Province of the Holy Ghost Congregation but they were already heavily committed to education in Ireland. Shanahan then decided to recruit diocesan priests and, given an opportunity to address a conference of Bishops in Maynooth, he is reputed to have spoken "as never before nor since"(Fr. J. Jordan). He followed this through by having his consecration as bishop in Maynooth, on June 6th 1920 and in this way released a wave of enthusiasm for missionary apostolates. In the years that followed Shanahan was to play a central role in the establishment of two Missionary Institutes – St Patrick's Missionary Society (1932), the Medical Missionaries of Mary (1937) – and was directly responsible for a third – the Missionary Sisters of the Holy Rosary (1924).

Back in Nigeria the idea of education for their children took a firm hold in the heart of the chiefs and through them the people. But now a new problem faced Bishop Shanahan. At the beginning, mostly boys were sent to school. He was quick to see that marriage of an illiterate woman to a literate husband would put the woman at a disadvantage. It soon became clear that a religious congregation of women would be needed to work for the women of Nigeria. And that is how the Congregation I joined came into being.

The Dominican Sisters at Cabra responded to his appeal to train the new Congregation. The Dominicans' strong monastic tradition was to influence the model of training and adaptations became necessary as the years went on.

Why was I becoming a nun? The reasons that I can remember in my inner core were entirely spiritual, or I thought they were. They crystallised during retreats in Balla when I felt that people 'out there' needed help more than people at home, and I promised I would give God not less than everything. That it was a difficult calling I was well aware, but that did not daunt me. That it entailed becoming a nun and wearing black stockings, which I detested, that it was a life commitment, leaving home, family, marriage, and career prospects forever, did not daunt me. If the thoughts of youth are long, long thoughts, the courage of youth needs another epithet. I bit it off and swallowed it whole. Its digestion and assimilation have taken much longer.

My call was missionary, to bring good news to the poor. Our Congregation's motto is: "Evangelisare pauperibus misit me" (He sent me to preach to the poor). This has never wavered. The religious life as a means to mission has taken a lot more querying. To be a missionary in those days was synonymous with being a Religious. If there was an option, like being a lay missionary, I might have taken it. Who knows? And why Africa? When my decision was upon me, in 1941-43, I knew almost nothing about any Congregation. The Far East magazine came to our house, so the Missionary Sisters of St. Columban, founded in 1922, was a possibility. I discussed it with the Mistress of Schools in Balla and she recommended Killeshandra. I took this as a sign that that was where I should go.

My poor Mother was devastated and fought hard to divert me. My father choked up as he said: "If it is what you want aghrá I wont stop you". He never commented again. Mother brought the parish priest on board who advised her to delay my entering the convent for six months claiming that the Far East had turned my head. It would pass, he said. So I capitalised on the situation by getting permission to go to the local dances. This was grudgingly given, but in view of the objective of the delay, was considered worthwhile. So keeping my intentions to myself, I danced up a storm for the six months and thoroughly enjoyed myself.

The Big Farewell: The day of departure came. I had received a very gracious letter from Killeshandra, excusing me from the necessity of an interview or a dowry, so I was really leaping in the dark. So was Holy Rosary of course!

It was February 1st, 1943. "Who will come with me?" I had asked and my mother had said: "He will go with you himself". Thus was my giving away formalised. My mother was inconsolable, having failed even to divert me to a home order, if I *had* to be a nun, which was not clear to her at all. My youngest brother was two years old. The rule in Holy Rosary then was that we would never go home again. God be praised, what a day! Everybody crying, the smaller children wide-eyed and uncomprehending. I stiffened my spine, made myself busy, and a tune went round in my head like some mad disembodied ghost in an attic: 'Good-bye old ship of mine'. At Westport Station, while my father, then over seventy years old, was stashing away the luggage, poor Mama's sobs got so loud that I called Dad's attention. He went quickly to the carriage door and said sternly: "Bridget! Bridget!" The train pulled out. It was the beginning of many a good bye, often as tearful as the first.

At Mullingar we were to spend the night. Such were the transport facilities in those days that it was impossible to travel from Mayo to Cavan in one day. Another aspect of the times was that it was not possible to phone ahead for reservations. Was there a telephone near us? Almost certainly there was not. Electricity reached The Colony in 1955, in time for my father's wake; direct dialling in 1987, in time for my mother's.

It was a Fair Day in Mullingar. It was the custom for cattle and sheep to be sold in the streets in those days. In the Midlands this was a crowded function and attracted farmers and 'jobbers' from all over the country. Therefore we found it difficult to find two rooms anywhere. "We will stay together, wherever we find a place", Father would say. Finally, we found a bed-and-breakfast type lodging where we were made welcome by an elderly couple. Conversation followed supper and in the usual exchanges it was discovered that our host bought sheep on a regular basis from Michael King, my father's brother-in-law in Leenane. Following this connectedness the nature of our business was told. They saw in this a repetition of the Little Flower, St. Therese of Lisieux, and her father going to Carmel. If standing on their grey heads could have helped us in any way they would have done it. God rest them. I cherish their memory.

Next day we proceeded to the railway station, looking now earnestly for one Vera O'Brien from Tuam, who, we had heard, would be 'entering' the same day. Affectionate, diminutive epithets were common in our 'breac gaeltacht' (breac means spotted and this

term was devised for areas where Irish was intermixed with English).
My father kept on saying:

"Look out, a ghrá, for that O'Brien girleen."

Perhaps he knew better than we did how much we had bitten off
and how much we would need each other. Be that as it may, at the
station I spied a large trunk and darted over to have a look at the
label, and there was "Miss N.V. O'Brien: Address: Killeshandra".
Her mother and Mrs. Swords, her mother's best friend, accompanied
her. We settled into the train. Excited exchanges:

"Who did you meet at the interview?"

"Didn't have one."

"Did you succeed in putting rubber soles on your shoes?"

"Did you buy the 'combinations'?" in reference to the incredible
underwear that was on the prospectus. If people thought our
outside robes were special, they should have seen our underwear.

Every now and then my father's eyes would fill and this had to
be prevented at all costs, for if he broke down, I was undone. So I
told yarn after yarn and kept them laughing. This was to have
consequences. Arriving at the convent, we were met by the Mother
General and the local Superior of Killeshandra Convent – and
Mother C. She was a beautiful looking lady, tall, graceful and
willowy, with lovely dark features. Her clothes hung gracefully
upon her, as if she were in evening dress. Being a country girl, her
very presence and bearing intimidated me. I was used to nuns in
black, but those lovely cream habits, falling in straight folds from
the shoulders, made me wonder if I had come to the right place. To
clinch it all, when the time of parting came, Mrs. Swords said: "Well,
I am cheered leaving them. They will never be dull, for this one
here (she indicated me) is better than Jimmy O'Dea." O'Dea was a
comedian of those days, and by today's standards would be very
respectable, but was he a recommendation for a prospective member
of the Missionary Sisters of the Holy Rosary? I could see Mother
wondering if a new edition of Jimmy O'Dea was at all necessary or
useful for Africa.

The relatives left. At a small ceremony that evening we made an act of consecration to the Apostolate and were presented with a black dress, a cape, and a black lace frilly cap. My training in the religious life had begun.

Beginnings: During the first phase of the training I was designated a Postulant; it lasted six months. During this time, I was eased into the format of the day by a white veiled novice, assigned to guide me and appropriately called, 'The Angel'. My angel was Mary O'Connor, at that time called Sr. Mary Addolorata. The name was impressive. She led me gently, telling me that I should arise at the second bell in the morning, which gave me half an hour extra sleep. I joined the larger community in chapel for meditation, followed by Mass. At about eleven o'clock, I joined the novices for ten mysteries of the Rosary, recited outside, come hail or shine. One bitterly cold day, the leader called out: "The Agony in the Garden". "This is it" said an irreverent postulant behind me. There was Scripture study, spiritual reading in private and in common. Meals in the very large refectory were eaten in silence, while lives of the saints or other spiritual books were read to us. There was recreation for one hour after the midday and evening meal. We talked, or did mending or, in the afternoon when it was dry, walked around the grounds, almost always accompanied by the novice mistress or her assistant.

Letters both in and out were opened, even those from our parents. My angel broke the news to me that we did not eat, or even drink water, between meals and we were to be silent except at recreation. There were no 'elevenses' heard of then (1943-45). Someone got a box of chocolates and was told to give it up, which meant giving it to the Superior, who gave it to the Bursar, who put it in the common store, for special occasions. And I had to be in time for everything. The sound of the bell was the 'Voice of the Lord' my angel said, so I believed her and did my best. I asked my friend at recreation: "How are you doing? Did you break silence today?" "No", she said, "I was real good." But then: "I get no kick outa being good; do you"? I assured her that the silence was just about killing me but sure we were here now and we had better give it a little longer. She did not stay.

We seemed to have a lot of set prayers and in between, there was reading, studying and chores. One postulant wrote home to say that she would be unable to fulfil promises of prayers for people, as there simply was no time for prayers of her own. She got that letter back.

I threw myself into the life as presented to me and, on the whole, enjoyed the postulancy. I had, I believe, during that time a significant conversion. I remember where I was sitting, reading Edward Leen's *In the Likeness of Christ*, when it struck me in a special way, as never before, that God became a human being; that he broke into human history, becoming one of us so that we might become him. The Latin expressed this mystery so well: "O admirabile comercium". It could be translated into modern jargon as "Awesome Deal". I was so delighted that I told the novice mistress that I understood all about the spiritual life now and that I had come to stay. She tartly reminded me that the congregation reserved the right to accept me. "Oh" I told her airily "that would not matter – I could practice my inner life anywhere" That light supported me through many a dim day.

Throughout the postulancy I struggled to learn Latin, which I had not done in school, so that I would enjoy the psalms, and scripture, and Gregorian chant and be ready for the novitiate.

Novice, Name and Habit: The Noviciate began with a moving ceremony, called 'The Reception'. It meant you were formally received as a prospective candidate and you received the official habit of the congregation, without the black veil. The novice wore a white veil. On the day, we were dressed in bridal dress and veil, representing all the good and beautiful things of the world, which we had chosen to leave behind. Kneeling at the altar, we were asked what we desired. Having stated that we wished to be formally received as novices, and our wishes being granted, we filed out of the chapel to put on the habit, never again to wear civilian clothes. Awkward and fumbling in the unfamiliar robes, we trundled back to the chapel for prayers and blessings – and to be given a new name.

"You Mary Lyons", I heard, holding my breath, "will be called Sister Mary Hilary". "And you Nora Veronica O'Brien will be called Sister Mary Lucy". Well, I thought, we have done well. Some received the names of Italian or Irish men saints from the Middle Ages or before. There was an Irish Saint called Fursey. Who wanted to be called Sister Mary Fursey? At that time we were not consulted. It seems strange that we abandoned our baptismal names, those names to which we first answered, which first set us apart from everyone else, and in my case which my mother had so specifically chosen for me, and adopted a new one. Many regretted this and resumed their original names when the changes came after Vatican II. I did not. By that time I was at home with 'Hilary'. Lucy has remained 'Lucy'.

The next days were spent getting used to the clothes. There was an inside shift, then the habit itself, which was cream serge and, as habits went, was not too voluminous. There were wrist length wide sleeves worn for chapel, parlour or going to see mother mistress of novices. There was a scapular, which is a long piece of material hanging from the shoulder to mid calf both back and front. At the neck a white, starched coiffe was worn. Mine used to turn around, or bump up in the middle at work and untidiness was not acceptable. The headdress was an oblong of linen, starched and hand folded so that the front part fitted along the forehead, a cap attached it to the head and the veil covered the lot. The mark of it is still on my forehead.

There were the black stockings. How I hated them. Woollen they were. They shrank in the laundry and grew little tufts on them and it became an increasing battle with gravity to hold them up. Corsets were then used and the suspenders got more and more extended, as the stockings got shorter. No bras, of course. We wore an indescribable white 'night coiffe' on our heads in bed, making us look like something one sees in a Dickens film.

In our general deportment we were to acquire a certain mien best described in Fr. Forrestal's *Second Burial of Bishop Shanahan:*

"Sisters were to walk, not run; to sit upright not slouch; to smile not to laugh loudly; they moved in a quiet and restrained manner, they kept their hands folded and their eyes modestly downcast, they avoided unnecessary looks or gestures. They ate what was set before them at meals and avoided taking as much as a drink of water between meals. As celibates they were to be particularly guarded in the presence of the opposite sex and even among themselves were careful to avoid any emotional relationships".

In this cloistered atmosphere there were: lectures in Scripture, Theology, Church History, Liturgy, the Rule and Constitutions and the Catechism of the Vows. It was the era of catechisms. Spiritual exercises were scheduled at regular intervals throughout the day; there was personal prayer, attention to all aspects of the Rule and a variety of household chores. All this demanded a rigorous discipline. Every activity of every day was scheduled and the schedule was to be followed by all, except in case of illness. We were not bound for a cloistered life, but for foreign countries, language, customs and climate.

An inner awareness of oneself and God's presence was to be practised assiduously. It was called recollection. I tried my very best to do this, determined to work, consciously and continuously, in an ambience of God's presence. I became so heavenly I was no earthly use. When I had responsibility for ringing the bell, I rang it late, or rang the wrong bell at the right time, or vice versa. This was serious, as the whole house-full of over one hundred women moved according to those bells. For penance I was obliged to take the responsibility for the bell for another week. I did – but rarely did any better.

Recreation was in common. We were expected to make conversational contributions of a lively, or learned nature. This was difficult, because we read nothing but the prescribed religious books. Radio, newspapers, or any contact with the outside world was not available. I was a great talker, with a fund of stories, and was much in demand by my more reserved Sisters, "to be there and say something". It was often, of course, not the right thing to say, or my elocution left a lot to be desired.

Many left during the noviciate and a number were de-selected. When someone left the noviciate, we were at once assembled. Quickly, one looked around for an empty chair. Sure enough, the novice mistress would enter, take her place at the top of the table and, still standing would say: "I wish to inform you that Sr. X has left the noviciate. You will not discuss this amongst yourselves, but pray for her that she will make the necessary adjustments." She then left and without a word we resumed our duties, sad because we had lost a friend and a little anxious, because we never knew if she was told to go, or chose to go. And whose turn tomorrow? I had so many corrections, for untidiness, forgetfulness, living in the clouds, that I had a period of anxiety as to whether I would be accepted. Then at a point I squared my shoulders and thought: " I can practice a spiritual life whether I am IN or OUT". So I felt better and waited. Anxiety is not easy to despatch, so I found myself scanning the faces of the members of the General Council who, I knew, would have received the file on my on going assessment from the novice mistress and would vote on my suitability for the religious life. My votes came through and I made profession of Poverty, Chastity and Obedience on August 28th 1945. Mother and Father and my two youngest sisters came for the ceremony.

4

To be a Doctor

For me this training began one day in 1945 when I had burned a batch of bread in the kitchen, and ended seven years later on the evening when Mother Brigid, the Superior General, assigned me to Sierra Leone. After profession of vows, a transition year was scheduled, in which we did not join the community of finally professed, nor did we belong to the noviciate any more. We were sandwiched between the two groups. We did not speak with them, except at work, nor did we recreate with them.

My assignment was to the kitchen. I was to cook the main meal for the community, over 100 people, bake the brown wholemeal bread and scrub the back kitchen. The latter, where food was prepared for cooking, usually needed a good scrubbing at the end of the day. The cooking facility was a long range, called the Esse, anthracite fuelled, with two large ovens and one small one. There were two fires, one between the small and first large oven and one between the two large ovens. The Esse was as temperamental as a mule, some days hot and some days luke-warm. The small oven was the prize as it always heated beautifully. One had to be crafty to get the use of it first.

I was also studying Latin for matriculation, and used to pop my Latin grammar on the shelf and recite: "mensa, mensa, mensam" while kneading the bread. On this particular day I put a batch of bread in the little oven and started the cleaning at the back. Alas, I dallied with the scrubbing brush and, when I opened the oven, cumuli of blue-black smoke billowed happily to the roof. Ashamed of my carelessness, distressed for the ruined bread, I was already upset when someone chose that moment to make a little caustic comment on my feather-headedness. The Sister in charge suggested that maybe I could be more serious about my work. Since the option of fighting back was not in my repertoire of responses at that time, I cried. I cried and I could not stop. Alarm on all sides. It was suggested that I go to the chapel and do my half hour spiritual reading and relax and I would feel much better. I did. I came back. As soon as I entered the kitchen I cried again.

With my two eyes like bruised tomatoes, that was the day I was told that the Mother General wanted to see me. My God! Had four pieces of whole-meal bread sent smoke signals that far? She bade me be seated and began:

"I will be out of the country for the next few months and would like to arrange the studies before I leave." In those days the studies were arranged and the sister's names and courses posted on the bulletin board. "We have decided to send you to study Medicine and in view of the nature of the studies, you are invited to say if you feel any particular repugnance to this assignment." I said I was not aware of any and I would do my best. Anything for Africa. No memory is now with me, as to whether I felt proud, or honoured to be asked to do Medicine, or if I had wished the chosen course had been English and History. That damn burned bread was all I could think of. When the subject was not coming up I said: "Is that all Mother?"

"Yes", she said. "What more do you want?" So the bread story was told – just that I burned a batch. She looked at me in a kind, amused, speculative way and said slowly: "Yes. Yes. All your reports from the noviciate said you were living in the clouds. That's fine for the noviciate, but would you kindly come down to earth now, where the rest of us are and keep your two feet firmly planted there."

Then she said briskly: " Sister Mary Lucy will be joining you. You will be wearing secular clothes, of course, so for goodness' sake keep your hair nicely trimmed." The woman was Mother Brigid Ryan, one of our greats. She was one of those who went to Nigeria as a young woman to help Bishop Shanahan, having first done midwifery, which she detested. She sent me to do medicine, which I do not think I would have chosen, and where I have thrived. It was she who sent me to Sierra Leone, which I have loved; it was she who decided that I should continue as a generalist, when there was a proposal that I do ophthalmology, which I would not have liked, but did not say so. A woman whose decisions influenced my life in such a blessed way, has a cherished place in my heart and memory.

Apart from the decisions that came in her way of duty, she was a woman of great charm. She seemed to hold rules and regulations lightly, if reverently. Killeshandra, our Mother House, was a hot house for people reaching for perfection, interiorly and exteriorly. Profession ceremonies were always preceded by an eight day retreat, when the whole house would be immersed in silence, the reading in the refectory more deeply spiritual than usual; three lectures a day, sometimes wonderful, sometimes mediocre.

One evening, after a profession ceremony, we were all tired and hanging around seeing off departing guests with tired, plastic smiles. Brigid was then assistant general of the congregation. Looking round at us all, she suddenly threw out her arms and said to me: "Oh how I wish I could go, right now, to some wild and open spaces". This was typical of her ability to cross the age and seniority gaps, and splash a small Mount Tabor on a dull day. She had hardly finished before I assured her I knew the place. "Let's go", she said.

We got a car and headed for the wilds of Galway and Mayo, taking in Connemara, Dulough and Clew Bay. We had tea at my mother's and on a bright, crisp August evening, climbed Croagh

Patrick as far as the statue of St Patrick and there, beside a running stream, said together the Evening Prayer, Clew Bay spreading its islands at our feet. An unforgettable evening.

The one problem to be faced in connection with the medical school assignment was my mother. She had fixed ideas about what we would do and how we would 'turn out'. As a teenager she would advise me not to date different people, so that when I married there would be, would have been, only one man in my life, as if she had been reading Barbara Cartland. Later in life I saw her reading Hemingway. She must have learned a few things by then.

In her hierarchy of occupations, teaching occupied the top slot. Teachers, she figured, walked tall in their community. There were, of course, the expectations of a good steady job with a pension and holidays three times a year. Nursing or medicine? No! She had prayed furiously that either of these things would not happen to me. It happened. Not even the prestige value of being a doctor compensated for not being a teacher. And anyway, who would ever know I was a doctor out there in far away Africa.

So accepting the inevitable she turned her prayer batteries against my ever being sent to Sierra Leone, which she had heard, was once called "The White Man's Grave". When that did happen later, she argued with the Almighty that I should be allowed to die in Ireland.

Poor mother! She even came to dislike the entire African race feeling that in some way, incomprehensible to her, Africa and Africans had be-witched me.

We 'Come Out': It is almost impossible to describe or communicate, the sense of otherness that I, and my companions, had acquired, in the three and a half years we had been in the convent. There was the new name, the habit, and the universal restraint and modesty, with which we were expected to comport ourselves, at all times and in all places. The latter was particularly difficult for me and would need a powerful re-adjustment. I had been in and now was now coming out. But it was different.

Sr. Lucy and myself, and two sisters who were going to study Arts, got on the train at Cavan in September 1946. We created a convent around us, right there on the train, sitting two opposite two in silence. In due time, we took out the breviary, sat bolt upright on the outer third of the seat, back straight, chin in, four fingers lying on the back of the book and thumb on the lower edge, exactly as if we were in choir. We read the psalms for the feast of St. Michael the Archangel. Trains had a different design at that time. There were two seats opposite each other on either side, with a passage between them. We had not, of course, noticed a gentleman on the other side, who had taken out his sketchpad and done a lovely pencil sketch of Sr. Lucy at prayer. He handed it to her when we changed stations at Mullingar. Lucy was embarrassed but smiled charmingly as she accepted it. There was nothing that we could think of, in the Rule to cover such an occasion

Arrived in Dublin, the taxi service we chose was a horse and buggy. So we arrived at the door of 84 Lower Leeson St., where Lucy and I were to spend almost seven years.

Sr. di Ricci opened the door, and when we showed her the pencil sketch she said: "Oh, how exciting! Did you ask for his autograph?" Poor us. It looked like it was not going to be easy to be right. We thought we had done very well, to refrain from engaging in conversation with a strange man in the train. But we were back on earth now, and expected to behave like mature women, using good judgement, grace, and courtesy.

At that period nuns of all congregations were going to Universities. All the academic degrees were approved but care of the sick, especially midwifery and medicine, were only emerging from strict control by Rome. Norms for the Approbation of New Institutes, issued by the Holy See in 1901 and repeated in 1921, prohibited Religious from giving aid in childbirth and from attending women in maternity homes, while the Code of Canon Law, published in 1917, forbade the practice of medicine and surgery. When permission did come in 1936 it was laced with many injunctions and recommendations, one of which was, that medical students would wear a modest lay dress.

If the idea of lay dress was that we would not be seen to be nuns, it was naive. For one thing our clothes were modest, rarely changed in style and we never appeared at any social function or wore make up. We did not even appear at the hospital canteen for a cup of coffee. The students were quick to identify us as Sisters. Later, we resumed the full habit for our practice of medicine in Africa, in conditions where lay dress would have been much more appropriate.

I cannot now remember if we got any new clothes and cannot remember what Lucy wore. There was a rummage through the clothes that novices entered in and that had not yet been passed on to the poor, or sold in a jumble sale for the 'Missions'. Since everyone entered the convent with the intention of staying there, no one, or hardly anyone, came in their best, so we rummaged and took the best that fitted us. I only remember that I had a rather shapeless brown coat and a copper coloured satin scarf, with a peacock on the corner. The scarf lasted me the entire six and a half years. We were to cover our heads in the street, of course. On arrival at the door of '84', the house of studies, I would raise my hand to put the key in the lock and the scarf would slip off. Since it was only a short distance to the cubby-hole, where we donned a black dress and the full head gear, I got into the practice of passing through the hall with head uncovered. I was told this was an ominous sign of invading worldliness and possible loss of vocation.

Our stockings, were the same as the horrid black ones of former days only these were khaki-coloured. And they got short. And they developed bumps. Lyle was the eventual improvement on them. I don't think we made it to silk. But one lovely suit I did have, tailored by Sr. M. Andrew O'Shea for her final examination in Home Economics. It also lasted the course. When the 'new look' came in I put in a piece at the waistband and lengthened it. When the clothes got short I took the piece out again.

The fact that Lucy and I were in secular clothes was the occasion of our being chosen for a part in a Mission film being produced by Holy Rosary Sisters entitled "Out of the Darkness". It showed two young women, Lucy and myself, being interviewed as prospective postulants. We were, of course, professed nuns at the time. It continued with shots of us working in various places during our postulancy and noviciate, including shots of the reception of the habit, and actually went on location to Nigeria. There the scene was taken up with other 'Sister Stars'. It was a good film and, though it did not break any box office records, was shown in Dublin Cinemas and afterwards in halls and schools around Ireland.

Back in The Colony my brother Myles tells the story that the night the film came to Louisburgh, my hometown, everyone who had a bike made for the town from the hills and valleys. Since many did not have lamps on their bikes, an enthusiastic Gárda gave them a summons to court. When the case came up the Magistrate wondered how there could be so many involved on one night. When he heard the story he dismissed all of them. Myles also remembered that on that night he was left to finish the farming chores and found a calf had fallen into an unused limekiln. It had to be got out. The 'gassur' who was helping him was smaller than himself, so when Myles went into the pit to push up the calf, the small assistant was unable to grab and hold him up. Finally they got the calf out but were late for the show.

I enjoyed the filming too much and had to be cautioned for drawing attention to myself. The film is still available and it is a strange feeling to see oneself in that suit, aged 22. Hats were worn in those days on formal occasions. Needless to say we did not buy new ones. More rummaging among old clothes. Those we wore defy description. It was fun.

Eighty Four: The house of studies was situated at No. 84 Lower Leeson St., Dublin. It was ideally situated for students as it was within five minutes walk of both St. Vincent's Hospital and University College. ·

On returning to the convent, sister medical students were obliged to change into a black dress and the usual headgear. When going out on any business other than studies we wore the long black overcoat and headgear; thus we sometimes changed three times in a day. I hated those arrangements but said nothing. Complaining was not a virtue.

As far as possible the order of the house was the same as in the Mother House, with the exception of a dispensation from the recitation of one large part of the psalter. Apart from that, mass, meditation, reading, the profound silence at night, weekly confession, and silence through out the house were retained.

Study was unremitting. There was a piano, but no radio or newspapers unless a special article was picked out for us, and left in the library. The prevailing philosophy among Holy Rosary Sisters was that results were not to be worried about. If you did your best, but failed, you would accept it in a mature manner and wait to be told what to do next. If you succeeded, there would be no great celebration. In fact discipline demanded that, the night our final medical results came out, we would wait until morning to collect them. We did not obey that rule. Our good friend Miriam Brennan came and whispered our success into the profound silence.

In spite of everything we had fun – and lots of it. During the year we called 'second med' I developed a great interest in the dynamics of walking. I could imitate the walks of many of the sisters and the college lecturers. I would watch them coming into lecture, then, suddenly I knew I had it and thought I could even feel like the person.

In our basement kitchen, on many a cold winter's night over a hot drink, we medicos would congregate and laugh fit to burst, as we gave free shows on the people in our lives. There, also, unmentionable medical jokes could be exchanged. Like Mr. D. approaching a patient propped up for a haemorrhoid operation and pontificating with: "There's a divinity that shapes our ends!"

And so in that basement kitchen we regaled each other with

whispered medical ribaldries, the whole immensely garnished by the fact that it was 'profound silence' one floor up.

University College, Dublin: This was one of the three branches of the National University of Ireland. It was situated then in Earlsfort Terrace near lovely Stephen's Green. The course for the basic degrees in medicine, surgery, and obstetrics lasted for six and a half years.

I assume medical training has been revolutionised since then. The time frame was 1946 – 1952. Penicillin, streptomycin and cortisone were the wonder drugs of the time and were to change the face of medical practice, for the foreseeable future. Though news of great strides in therapeutics reached us daily, we were trained in the pattern of the vanishing pre-penicillin era: we were to be diagnosticians by use of eyes, hands, ears and the spoken word. Diagnostic technology was minimal compared to the present time.

It was to be three years before we got to the hospitals. Here was a world of excitement, of white coats and stethoscopes, of surgery, of hardworking men and women, geniuses and eccentrics, and the nuns who ran the hospital. Nurses, who in any hospital are the heart of the matter, flew around, little veils flying behind them. They seemed to know everything and were the people I felt would give me the useful tips I needed, and I was not wrong. We scrambled for clinical experience, attending clinics, surgery and laboratory when these functions were in session. In the afternoon there were on-going lectures in college and hospital chores had to be finished in time or the college just marked you absent.

On the discipline side in the hospitals the nuns ran a tight ship. Thrift and the economic use of resources stood head and shoulders above many virtues. One day, handing me a piece of equipment that had a lot of glass, sister cautioned me to be careful: "if you break it you will pay for it". The old man for whom the procedure was done, held the glass carefully with two hands and, when we were finished said: "Wash it, a ghrá, and give it back to her. If you'da broken it Id'a gone havers wid ye."

Throughout my student days I attended every procedure I possibly could, even those not particularly required of me, like dental work. I specially haunted the operating theatre, knowing that, in the far away places of the future, no learning would go to waste, and I might be able to help some suffering person, in circumstances where I would be the best available.

It would be three and a half years from the time of entering the hospital before I was allowed to do an appendicectomy under supervision and that only by kind courtesy of the late Bob O'Connell, who took an interest in me. Mr.O'Connell was a senior Consultant Surgeon in St. Vincent's at the time and as well as being a surgeon and lecturer, was a brilliant mimic and story-teller. He was also a rabid rugby fan.

His way of giving me confidence was to treat the event as if we were doing it every day. The patient was on the table and I knocked at the door of the surgeon's coffee room. "The patient is on the table, sir", I said. It seemed to me that the conversation in that room was always RUGBY. Waving a newly lighted cigarette in a wide arc, he pronounced what position Karl Mullen should play in the up coming rugby match. I groaned inwardly. Does he not know that this is the day? Does he not know that I have gone over every single step of this procedure, one hundred times over the last twenty four hours, that I went to bed with it, got up with it and now all the attention I am given is Karl Mullen's position on the rugby field. Karl Mullen indeed! "Scrub up", he shouted, "I'm coming", and he went on with his rugby business. I went back and started scrubbing. I scrubbed and I scrubbed, because I would neither begin by myself nor would the anaesthetist give the anaesthetic until the boss was there. After what seemed an hour, and was probably two minutes at most, he bustled in, plastic apron flapping, groaning in a low hollow voice: "Oh God! I thought you would be finished by now". I took my place at the table. I was very confident that I knew how to do it. I had assisted at so many. No problem. But, when I had put on the sterile towels and looked at the small area that was exposed, my courage deserted me.

It looked as large as a football field. Suddenly, this was human skin in front of me and I – myself – was about to apply a knife to it.

"Lord" I prayed desperately "how heavy do I lean on this blade?" "Don't" I urged myself idiotically, "go out through the man's back"

Ready to make the incision, and having measured correctly the incision line, but needing a teeny-weeny bit of encouragement, I looked up, scalpel in hand, and pleaded: " 'Bout here?"

"Don't know", he said wickedly.

The anaesthetist asked the boss, courteously, if the position of the table was OK for him. " I don't know how she wants it. I am not doing this job"

I thought, "By golly, I'll show him". Fore finger and thumb of left hand stretching the skin a little, in the surgeon's special pose, I drew the scalpel, and surveyed the damage. There was a pathetic shallow little scar with a few tiny red spots in the base looking sadly up at me.

"You'll draw blood if you're not careful", says himself. Next stroke took me through to the fascia and after that I went sailing. But I was slow, and later the ward sister fixed me with a beady eye and asked: "Was that an uncomplicated appendix?" If she knew that I had done it there was big trouble in store for me. Young doctors were, to her, the greater of the necessary evils.

The other place we flocked around was the outpatient department. There the patient who had a heart or lung lesion would be listened to over and over. God knows they were patient with us. It was up to us to get all the experience we could, and fit our lectures in as well.

Obstetrical experience was the only course where 'live-in' was obligatory.

In the summer term of 1951 Lucy and I took up residence in The National Maternity Hospital, Holles Street. Nurses, as well as medical students, trained there. Each student was obliged to conduct a prescribed number of normal deliveries under supervision as well as attend and/or assist at surgical interventions.

Although there were a great number of deliveries, delivery room staff was not going to go to great trouble waiting for students, if they were not near at hand. The time of a delivery being of its nature uncertain, it was important to keep an eye on what was brewing in the delivery room. The nurses had the advantage over us, because they received assignments to the delivery room and consequently were in a better position to scoop up the 'cases'. For some reason three of us women medical students were located in the nurses quarters, which meant that we could ask the nurses to call us at night, for either a delivery or surgery.

We also attended the large antenatal clinics where we learned how to hear a foetal heart, how to identify the position of the baby and many other skills. The total health of the mother was always emphasised as the pre-condition for a healthy baby.

Missing from the overall curriculum at that time was any form of training in domiciliary practice, which, for most students, would be part of their practice. I do not remember a home visit. No one mentioned who paid the bills, or how the cost of medical care affected the national economy, or the individual patient. Both of these items were important for work in Africa. Health Economics has since become a major issue in Western economies.

On the clinical side I was ill prepared for the problems of human sexuality and sexually transmitted diseases that I was obliged to manage very early in my clinical life. There was no training in research methodology of any kind. This was a great pity. Nevertheless, in spite of that, the training was rich in 'patient first' care, in using all our faculties, speech, sight, hearing and touch in establishing a diagnosis. This was most valuable for me later in Africa, where I had so little diagnostic facilities, and where, thankfully, establishing a doctor/patient relationship is still an essential component of medical practice.

Grand old gentlemen of medicine graced the corridors. They would respond to the avalanche of new drugs coming on the market with: "I am never the first to drop an old medicine and never the last to accept a new one" of Dr. Meenan. Or "the new poison " of Mr. Morrin.

It was a busy life.

In his book, *The Youngest Science*, Lewis Thomas comments on the use of modern medical technology such as transplants, in vitro fertilisation, cloning, genetic engineering, scans and MRI's. He reflects that the loss of close personal contact today between patient and doctor, may eventually be calculated in more than dollars and cents. He writes:

"There are costs to be faced. Not just money, the real and heavy dollar costs. The close reassuring warm touch of the physician, the comfort and concern, the long leisurely discussions, in which everything including the dog can be worked into the conversation, are disappearing from the practice of medicine and this may turn out to be too great a loss, for the doctor as well as for the patient."

He continues that if he were now a medical student he would be apprehensive:

"That my real job, caring for sick people, might soon be taken away leaving me with the quite different occupation of looking after machines."

A road sign in Sierra Leone, which read "DANGER, ROAD WORKS IN PROGRESS" fell down once and when it was re-assembled the middle board was missing. It then read "DANGER IN PROGRESS". It may be that this applies to high technology in health care.

Stresses and Strains: In spite of returning to the Mother House and convent life during holidays it was, I suppose, inevitable that what I thought was my spiritual life, would have taken a beating by the end of medical school. The first time that I resided outside the convent was during the residence period in the National Maternity Hospital. There I enjoyed normal social life with my peers and threw myself in to the fun, give-and-take of ordinary student life. The exuberance and enjoyment of life, which is natural to me, returned. There were a few of the men students getting away with too many practical jokes on the women, so Lucy and I decided to take a hand.

No one would suspect us. So when one or two of the students were in theatre or delivery room out of turn, we stitched up the inside of the sleeves of their jackets and embroidered daisies on the lapels. One guy accosted me on the corridor demanding to know if I were the culprit. I drew myself up to my full forbidding religious 5'2" and said in great disapproval: "Frank!" It contained, "Remember who you are talking to. There are certain limits."

"I – I'm sorry – Sister", he conceded and let me go by. But I had not gone far when, "I don't know all the same", was hurled at my departing back.

The sequel was that I got blamed when I was not guilty. One famous day someone took Dr. M.'s shoes while he was in theatre. He caught my two wrists and shook me, saying: "I don't care if you are a religious. I don't care how long you are in religion. I MUST have my shoes – I have a date". I stood helplessly disclaiming all responsibility until the culprit was found.

It was a Sunday and we were going home to '84'. It was a Retreat Sunday, silence all day, and it was difficult to enter into a worshipful mood. Lucy said wearily: "I wonder do they understand in '84' about the two life styles we live?" And that said it all. It was summer time, rhododendron time, and lilac time. The students went into the square, played tennis, or lay on the grass to read a book, or picked daisies or whatever. But we went home to silence, the black dress and the head gear and the rules that made little sense, e.g. if we wore the full habit and wanted to go down town we had to go in twos, though we could be up all night with students in the hospital.

The students were an exceptionally friendly group. We moved among them with ease and confidence and I never remember being deliberately embarrassed by anyone. Teased, yes. At the beginning I was dismayed to discover that I developed 'crushes' on some of the guys. After all that praying and recollecting and all, I'd thought I'd be DIFFERENT DAMMIT! Not quite human. However my heart did not break and, by the end of the course, I had developed a few close friendships; the memory of these I carried with me to Africa. I have not kept in touch with those friends, as I would have liked to; life swells up like an ocean and carries us all on our different ways, leaving only memory currents to connect us.

At the end of our time in Holles Street we went to the Mother House in Killeshandra and were given time for study. This was a great concession as we normally worked the whole holidays, in the kitchen or poultry farm. Now we went from large medical tomes to prayer, meditation and meals in silence. The difficulty of trying to make two worlds mesh began to tell. The two worlds of course were within as well as without me. Life had provided me with natural gifts of humour, repartee and light heartedness, and medical school provided a forum for their growth. Had I become 'natural' as distinct from the 'supernatural' I was supposed to be? The duality on which I was trained was tearing me apart. Religious life seemed less attractive. Where now, I wondered disconsolately, was recollection, where was the joy that prayer and prayers had always brought me? My emotional life descended into a bleak greyness, where there was no light and no exit. I wondered if I was indeed coming apart. Who to ask? No one. They might tell me I had no vocation and I did not believe that. I did mention it to a priest in confession and he told me, it was a common experience for people returning from the rarefied atmosphere of the noviciate, to real life.

And anyway, I thought to myself, Africa is in my sights now and that is what it was all about in the first place so I am not giving up.

I pressed on and, at the end of that holiday, made perpetual vows of Poverty, Chastity and Obedience and went back for the final year. All that year I just stumbled on, on the outside telling stories, and, as they say, "keeping the best side out". I used to look at myself and say: "Which one is me. Will I flip?" I did not. I did my internship in surgery and was assigned to Africa. That year in final medical school was the hardest year of my life so far. In Africa I have known frustration, betrayal, tears and laughter, and sometimes all in one day, but never have I known a day's depression as I had then. The words of

Eibhlis N. Sullivan on leaving the Blaskets occur to me: " . . . Whatever happens on this Island I have one gifted thing to tell you of it. I was always happy there. I was happy among sorrows".

In many ways Africa made me. Or re-made me?

Lucy at prayer in the train 1946

5

Africa Calling

The long day of training and waiting for Africa was coming to a close. I enjoyed my internship immensely. The exams were behind me. There was real responsibility, friendships and camaraderie. In '84' also we had developed great friendships with student sisters studying other disciplines. And soon there would be Africa. Where? Most likely Nigeria where Holy Rosary had a rapidly growing number of established works. It would be the most likely place as there were other doctors there for the initial orientation. However, fears about the newly opened 'medical work' in Sierra Leone would pass before me darkly, but I don't deny without an element of excitement.

One night I stopped Lucy on the stairs. "Tell me", I said, "what would you do if you were assigned to Sierra Leone?"

"Lady", she said – or words to that effect – "Since it's not going to happen to either you or me, why worry?" Sensible woman was Lucy.

One night in January I came home from the hospital rather late and met Mother Brigid near the dining room door. This room was in the basement and I had a sudden quick intuition that the Mother General was not loitering around the basement without intent. She asked if she could see me for a moment. "Oh ho!" said I to myself, "This is it".

"I am sending you to Africa", she said simply.

I replied in Latin: "Benedictus Deus in donis suis" (Blessed be God in all his gifts), which was the standard response on these occasions whether the assignment was to the kitchen, the poultry farm, or far away places with strange sounding names never heard of before. Obedience was almost military in its application in those days. To day, there is an element of dialogue built into it. However, in this case I was being very well treated. Normally, as previously said, the names and destinations were put on the bulletin board.

We were standing. Now she moved a chair in my direction. Excitement growing by the second I said: "Do you reckon I need a chair for the rest of it Mother?"

"I reckon you might", she said. "I'm sending you to Sierra Leone"

I don't remember what I said then. I was so excited, scared, delighted, emotions rollicking around pummelling me from every side like some mad jacuzzi.

She enquired kindly if I had had my supper and whether I was tired. Declaring that at that moment I was neither hungry nor tired, we sat down and had a good chat. She told me what she knew of Sierra Leone, advised me to keep in touch with the St. Joseph of Cluny doctor who was already in Sierra Leone and had been in the year before me in college.

Lucy did not receive her assignation the same evening. When she did it was to Nigeria where she was to do Trojan work until the outbreak of the Biafran war in 1967. Finding herself back in Ireland she used the time to study for, and obtain, her Membership of the Royal College of Obstetricians and Gynaecologists; she had a vast experience of Obstetrics and Gynaecology while in Nigeria. In the early 70's she came to me in Serabu during which time I escaped to study for a Masters in Public Health. Her next assignment was to Monze in Zambia where she has become a legend for her skill, commitment and dedication. In recent years she has been awarded an Honorary Fellowship of the College of Physicians of Ireland.

My departure date was towards the end of that same month, so I received permission to go home to say good-bye. My father was then 80. Since the rule was still in vogue that we did not stay in our own homes I was to make arrangements to stay in the local Convent of Mercy in Louisburgh. They were welcoming and supportive. Most of my relatives trooped into the convent during my two-day visit. I was taken for a drive to all the old places including my old home but could not enter it. Mrs O' Toole (Mary Davy John of long ago) reminded me recently that her mother was sick at the time and unable to come out to the car to meet me. She walked to the window, lifted up the curtain and waved. And then came the good-byes. I can still see my father's sad eyes looking at me all the time as the car drove away. Was there reproach there? We were not to meet again. These scenes left tears in my very soul.

But the young are resilient and as my much loved Croagh Patrick, Mweelra, Ailmore and the Twelve Bens slid away behind the bus, I dried my tears and turned my thoughts to the immediate problem of reaching Killeshandra in that same day. The bus I was in would take me to Longford; there I would take another bus to Cavan and there I would phone the convent, some 14 miles away, to send a car for me.

All went fine until the Cavan/Killeshandra limb. Apparently whoever got the telephone message in the convent forgot about me. In Cavan it was a cold, wet January evening and I took refuge in an office that was still open. The boss was still at his desk and I perceived him to be a little the worse, (or the better), for a few drinks at the Longford fair. "You're famished", he commiserated. "Take off your shoes and warm your feet".

Vast impropriety, but he was quite assertive in his cups, so I took off my shoes. He sent for a box of chocolates and when, good little nun that I was, I put it away to carry home, to 'give it up' he roared at me:

"Arn't you going t' ate it?"

"Now?" I said.

"Wha' the hell d'you think I bough' it for?" Hiccup! "Sorry, Sisther".

If I looked out to check for the car he would adjure me to "welax" and send someone to "sheck" outside. He dozed for a few minutes, then lifted his head, got me in focus and communicated to me his considered opinion:

"You know", he said, "You Killeshandra nuns are a crow' o' bloody shnobs".

In vino veritas. And as we were all professionally trained for our particular jobs it was just possible that there was a trace of exclusiveness amongst us. It is also possible that the man had little time for the rules and regulations that we carried about with us like not eating the chocolate he gave me. I told the story when I reached Killeshandra. Appreciative of the value of that kind of feed-back and its possible necessity, Mother Brigid loved it

Setting Sail from Liverpool: Packing, saying goodbye, travelling was the excitement as 1952 drew to a close. I knew virtually nothing about Africa or Africans beyond a few anecdotes told by returning missionaries. Missiology was a word not heard of in those days.

As soon as I received my assignment, preparations started. Six habits were sewn, in white cotton material, plus white lisle stockings. I packed breviaries including the large Liber Usualis that contained the music and words for Gregorian Chant. Household goods, school materials, church supplies, medicine and equipment were packed in tea chests labelled with paint. Before you left you knew how many pieces you were responsible for and you counted these at destination, and also at the change over at Liverpool. We crossed by Irish Ferry on January 30th, 1953 and boarded M.V.Tamele in the Mersey. It was a cold, grey January day. The Tamele was an old vessel overdue for retirement but during the immediate post war years, anything reasonably sea worthy still sailed. She was basically a cargo ship and carried a limited number of passengers. There were three bunks to a cabin. We were content. There were five of us, two going out for the first time, three returning to their mission. For Helen King and myself it was a first. We were lonely but did not say so. After a few days she and I repaired to an upper deck where deck chairs were stored and confessed to each other that all we could see were miles and miles of sweet nothing. Then we sang songs of Ireland and, if a tear or two fell, sure what harm – no one saw us. We ate with everyone else, a great departure from custom. Habits were found cumbersome for going up and down narrow stairs. Taking a turn on deck with the wireless operator on a windy evening, my back scapular flew around his waist. I had no sooner retrieved it than the front one flew around his chest. Lord bless us! I took some comfort in the belief that a Glenamaddy man would hardly think I was making advances.

Other than us there was a mixed group on board – some business people but colonial officials mostly.

There had been some trouble on board and we felt that a young steward had been unfairly treated by a domineering London businessman. So our first action on arriving in Freetown was to write to the manager of the shipping company giving our side of the story. I often wonder if we saved his job. It was the same businessman who, during the trip, took me to task for wasting my life in Sierra Leone and offered to find me a good job in England

Now I look back in awe at the memory of those days when, a graduate of the Penny Catechism, the Catechism of the Vows, and an MB from U.C.D. I shipped for Africa loaded with good news for the mind, soul and body of those 'poor Africans'. There were to be surprises ahead.

Africa at Last: After ten days The Tamele docked in Freetown, the third largest natural harbour in the world. While it was still dark I was on deck waiting for dawn and my first glimpse of Sierra Leone. Gradually, the hills of Freetown rose in silhouette against a paling sky and I recalled that it was this sight that moved the Portuguese to name the country in the sixteenth century. Some say that they thought the sound of thunder was the roaring of lions and others that the shape of the mountains looked like a lion or lions couchant. They mount guard over the city which lies scattered at their feet almost in the ocean. The heat was incredible. The number of black people swarming around claimed and reclaimed my attention; some were officials; many were dockhands, labourers, and porters carrying what seemed mighty loads on their heads. Happy people, talking, laughing; some bored, waiting for the next thing to happen, stretched out and went to sleep. These scenes were to become forever part of my life.

I lodged that night as we did many times later in St. Joseph's Convent, Freetown. I shall always remember, on my first night in Freetown, wondering if the heat was what I was to expect every day or if it was just a freak hot day. Turning and turning in the hot, moist bed looking for a cool spot but there was none. Long before dawn I was down in the quadrangle of the convent for morning meditation. I have only to stand there for a moment today, to re-experience the humid heat, to see again the stars give way to the opalescence of dawn, to see palm trees silhouetted against the approaching morning and to savour the sensation of pleasant strangeness as familiar scenes of Ireland faded out and Africa emerged to claim its place in my life.

The next day I spent in Freetown with Breed O'Keeffe, who had come to meet me, presenting passports to be stamped, obtaining work permits, and finally, visiting the shops. Nice shops. I had no feeling at all. I just went wherever I was taken, wondered about the heat, and nothing more. It was a bewildering world. No previous life experience I ever had felt at all relevant.

As our destination was Bo, 150 miles away, my companion and I set off by train on the third day. The train station was at the end of the present Malama Thomas Street and travelled the length of the street before going out of the city. I tried to see everything all at once, as if it were going to disappear. I saw a man pass us by on a bicycle. There were men loading and unloading trucks, carrying bags of cement, sacks of grain and large crates on their heads.

Women carried market produce on their heads and babies on their backs. I saw a woman with a bucket of water on her head and a baby on her back and she walked like a queen. Shops were opening, some were large buildings and some were just market stalls. Soon enough we were out in the country. I saw little houses with thatched roofs and mud walls, while others were zinc roofed. There were flowers and trees I had never seen before: wildly rioting pink, white or red bouganvillaea, scarlet hibiscus, frangipanni, pride of Barbados and dozens of others that were to be greatly loved as time went on. When we arrived at a station hoards of traders, mainly women and children, swarmed around the train pushing their wares. "Banana de go! Ground nut de go"! To make sure you understood, these items were pushed right into the carriage window.

As the day wore on and we stopped interminably at station after station in a conveyance that had now become an oven, heat and tiredness took over. At about 8 p.m. the train stalled somewhere between Yamandu and Gerihun. There we sat till 10.30 p.m. while the mosquitoes feasted on us. It was late when we pulled into Bo. The sight of the convent, the first foundation we had in Bo, was blessed. There followed a wash, a cuppa and to bed. I had finally arrived.

Sierra Leone is a small Ireland-sized country with roughly the same population. Only eight to ten degrees north of the Equator, it is extremely hot. Its immediate neighbours are Liberia and Guinea. The heavy rainfall between May and October, together with the dense tropical bush growth and some fine forests, create a high humidity and a trying climate. The country is hilly rather than mountainous except in the North, and though the hills and sea at Freetown are reminiscent of Western Ireland the rest of the country varies, mostly having gently rolling hills separated by fertile valley swamps. There are several large rivers, which flow from N.E. to S.W. breaking into a fish-rich network of tributaries before entering the ocean.

Sierra Leone is very rich in minerals such as bauxite, titanium, iron ore, gold and diamonds. Gem diamonds of high quality occur alluvially along main river basins. In spite of all efforts to control the illicit mining of these precious gems, it is almost impossible to do so in the thick jungle. The presence of diamonds is a mixed blessing.

The country has great agricultural potential: rice (the staple crop), cassava, yams, sweet potato, palm oil, cocoa and coffee abound; there is a great variety of citrus and a large riverine and ocean fishing industry.

There are some eighteen ethnic groups, all speaking different languages, but the two main groups numerically are the Mende in the South and the Temne in the North. The main religions are Islam, (40%) and Christianity (10% of which 2% is Catholic). Traditional religion (50%) is still a living force.

Sierra Leone is a country of great natural beauty. There are rivers, waterfalls, and lakes; some prime forest, and a lot of bamboo; all the tropical foliage, flowers and birds you can think of; and there are clean miles of tourist dream beaches, all making this one of the world's lovely countries.

On the negative side there are a great number of microorganisms hostile to humans. The snail, which harbours the schistosome, – the organism responsible for Bilharzia – lies among the water lilies. Mosquitoes breed in quiet pools and make malaria still a major killer. Simulium Damnosum, a black fly so-called because its bite is so painful, is the carrier for filaria, the organism causing river blindness. It needs fast flowing water to breed. It is clear that the control of those two vectors would be a great breakthrough, but it is not yet in sight. There are a great variety of intestinal parasites to be picked up; leprosy is endemic, as are cholera, typhoid, and tuberculosis. With poor salaries, sometimes not paid for months, poor roads, low agricultural yields, good land chewed up for mining purposes, and health services receiving little of the budget, there is no great hope for a change in health status in the foreseeable future.

Mercifully I did not know anything about these factors in 1953. I was full of hope and indeed there was hope in the very air.

In the post World War II period, colonised countries worldwide wanted independence. Sierra Leone was no exception. The colonising country had been Britain. Only the present Western Area (Freetown) and Bonthe was a colony, the rest of the country being a protectorate. The Protectorate was administered jointly by UK Colonial Officials and a Protectorate Assembly, which comprised educated members of the community and in particular Bo School alumni. Bo School was set up in colonial times mainly for the sons of chiefs and other upper class members of the society.

By 1950 the outline of independence was fairly well defined and Sierra Leoneans were making plans in that direction. One such was Dr. M.A.S. Margai. He was a retired Sierra Leonean Medical Officer and had set up a private nursing home in Bo on Ngalu Road, near the present Queen of the Rosary (Q.R.S.) Secondary School for Girls.

Though Dr. Margai studied medicine in Britain, he never strayed far from his roots in Sierra Leone. On returning to his country he was quick to perceive the need for training of Traditional Birth Attendants and wrote a primer for this exercise. He was way before his time in this.

As his political ambitions developed he approached the Catholic Mission, in the person of the late R. B. Kowa, who was a prominent and respected member of the Catholic Church and also an aspiring politician, asking if a doctor could be provided to help him run his hospital while he tested out whether his political star would rise or set. I was given that assignment and thus had the honour of receiving my orientation to Sierra Leone from its first Prime Minister.

Sierra Leone gained political Independence from Britain in 1961. I was there for eight years of colonialism. People ask me "What was it like?" The colonial era vanished to such an extent that it is really difficult to believe it ever existed, though many of the traditions of the British way of life lived on. My memories are of expatriate personnel in virtually all senior posts in the civil service and business fields. Most of them would have been British, but French, Swiss and

Indian nationals were also there in smaller numbers promoting their country's interests. Lebanese were the trading middlemen, situated mainly, but not entirely, in the rural areas.

The senior civil servants were the cream of society, big fish in a small pond. They spoke with educated English accents and manned provincial and district posts as well as all the various ministries in Freetown. The Government model set up was, of course, British. We held Government officials in some awe as they determined how the health and educational services would be run – these were the two areas where we were involved. Actually we, on the ground, had little enough dealings with such officials. What little we had convinced us that they were snobbish and somewhat anti-Catholic. This perception may well have had its origin in our own prejudices and those current at the time. Our meetings would have been on the periphery of official occasions like visits of the District or Provincial Officers where we sang "God save the Queen" – Irish tongues in cheek!

As individuals, the colonials worked hard. They had a good social life, especially in Freetown. As I went shopping I could see the ladies stepping it out to the 'Cold Store', the supermarket of the time, followed by their cook and/or houseboy. On my occasional visits to Freetown I could see them having an early morning game of tennis; see them on the beach browning to a turn as I paddled in my bare feet, which was all that was allowed in those days. There was some class distinction, even within the colonial ranks, senior civil servants being the upper classes and those in the commercial sector a little below. Graham Greene uses this social inequality with great poignancy in *The Heart of the Matter*. From our point of view as missionaries the commercial people were helpful and friendly. We did business with them and we got to know each other. How did they see us? Later when we were in Serabu, a pharmacist in Kingsway, one of the leading stores, was to say to Sr. Anita and me: "Look! You two! Up there in that bush! What fine wives and mothers you would have been". Then he grinned and said: "I think you're crazy – nice crazy – but crazy all the same."

I had arrived in a country, which was managed and administered by a colonial power and it was within this context that our missionary work was carried out. The Church itself must have looked like another hierarchy within the colonial system, and in retrospect I often wonder what the people of Sierra Leone thought of us all. I was told a story of a chief, who had missionaries in his chiefdom at the time of the hut tax war and, when asked what was to be done about them, said: "We do not know what good they do but since they do not do any harm leave them alone".

6

The Margai Nursing Home

Two days after my arrival in Bo I was introduced to my first place of work, where I was to spend a year and a half. It was a small hospital or nursing home in Bo that Dr. Margai had asked us to run, while he embarked on a political career. He was, in fact, to become the first Prime Minister of Independent Sierra Leone, was later honoured by the Queen and called Sir Milton Margai.

The hospital was a single story mud building, neatly plastered over with cement. When I climbed the front steps and entered the wide front door, I found myself in a large hallway, which stretched across the width of the building and opened out to the back. On my left was a ten bed women's ward, with similar accommodation for men on my right. Two smaller places cut off from the large rooms served for dispensary and consulting rooms respectively. Beaten zinc made adequate doors, security not being a problem in those days. Cement floors were yielding up clouds of dust to a raffia broom in the hands of Jabbati, the cleaner. The beds were narrow, low and had a minimum of covering. The patients were cautious about this young white 'titi' (young girl) being introduced to them, instead of their reliable and well-loved Doctor Margai. Out back was the operating theatre, similar to the wards. There was a simple operating table, an instrument trolley, and a few drums, which, I assumed, contained sterilised material. I was a long way from St. Vincents.

"What do you think of it?" I was asked by older missionaries who always liked to hear what the 'new wan' said. If you were precocious you would have to live it down. You were expected to know nothing and learn from your betters.

Bereft of opinions I ventured cautiously: "Well, it's a beginning".

Turning to the task on hand, I asked the nurse: "Where are the instruments sterilised?"

I was shown three stones holding up a large pot. Firewood burned brightly beneath the pot, licking it to the brim and sending spirals of smoke to embrace the nurse, Dinah Peters. I still remember her name because she became my mentor in that strange new scene. She shed many smokey tears, blowing the fire to brightness, as she boiled the instruments and carried them to a tray, which she had already mysteriously sterilised. Mysteriously, because the tray was so much larger than the pot it was not clear how it got sterilised. But I was to learn that the less elaborate procedures were not necessarily more dangerous. For the moment I was bewildered.

The religious garb was again proving less than suitable. I wore a heavy rubber apron (no light plastics had yet appeared) over the robes, over that the sterile gown, and thus clad waddled to the operating table like a haystack. Fluid loss in perspiration was phenomenal. I was particularly lucky that my forehead did not sweat. It oozed out my neck, down my ribs and finally down my legs. If something was going down the leg it was perspiration. Carry on doctor. If something was going up it was a bug – holler! There was no air-conditioning. Surgery was done with open windows at first and Africa's wealth of insects flew around at will. Wire screening came later so that air could come in and the bugs stay out. Working in these conditions was wearing and it is probably true to say that representations about the unsuitability of the amount of clothes being worn came initially from the medical sisters.

As soon as we began work the numbers of patients increased and Dr Margai was requested to rent us his private home, which was on the compound. He agreed. This had a very large parlour where we put some eight beds in a row on one side and used a small room for surgery. It was very small. Another small room made an office. Being 'us' – white people and nuns – we started immediately to do up the place. Curtains, counterpanes and a big sign post at the end of the road read: THE MARGAI NURSING HOME

Doctor Margai, though pleased with the innovations, smiled and said: "These are your needs – not the Mende man's". This marked the beginning of what was to be a recurring theme in my missionary life: differentiating between what the people needed and what I thought they did. Dr. Margai was immensely helpful settling any 'palavers' (quarrels or disputes) that arose among the staff. We did some cases together and he showed me how to manage pathology I had not seen before. He would take time out, even from the Protectorate Assembly, to do a quick round with me. It was much later that I came to realise how privileged I was to have my first steps in Sierra Leone guided by the man who was to lead the country into independence and be its first Prime Minister. I was standing in history.

Kula: It was in 'The Margai' as we used to call it that I shed my first tears and laughed my first laughs. Kula was the occasion of the first. She was about sixteen years old and pregnant for the first time. She came from Tikonko, a large chiefdom, bordering the Kakua chiefdom where Bo is situated. She was either the niece or the daughter of the Paramount Chief.

The Paramount Chief is the traditional leader of his people and rules over a unit called the Chiefdom. This corresponds roughly to a county in Ireland. Ten to twelve such Chiefdoms make up a District. The population varies from quite small numbers like 4,000, in areas of low population density, to 60,000 in mining areas. Whether the area is small or large, the Chief is a very important person. A chiefdom Speaker and elders assist him, or her, (the chief may be a woman), to administer the territory. The chiefdom is subdivided into Sections and a similar hierarchy administers each section. All are responsible to the Paramount Chief. It could be described as an 'hierarchical democracy' where decisions are made by the chief, but with intensive dialogue and protocols of procedure.

Kula, as I have said, was a young girl in her first pregnancy. She had toxaemia and some cardiac complication. The details are a bit fuzzy now, but I decided to do a Caesarean section. Her heart stopped on the table. I directed the nurse to resuscitate and in seconds had the baby out. The baby lived. Kula did not. Any experienced surgeon will attest that there is nothing as soul shattering as a death on the table. I was devastated. This was my first Caesarean in Sierra Leone. I was devastated for a maternal death of a young woman in the prime of life. How was I to face the family? Although who she is, is not supposed to matter, it does a little bit. She was, after all, the chief's daughter. Also I was a little afraid. New in a new country, I had heard stories that if you had a death on the table in some cultures, you should have a fast exit ready. And as my mother would say we do not know 'these people'.

Nevertheless I told myself that these things happen and life goes on, and with other useless, comfortless thoughts, I went about the day's work as best I could

It was evening time when I reached the women's ward for rounds. The ward was only wide enough for one row of beds and they were on my left as I entered. The women sat up, as on cue, as I entered and I thought: "Oh my God, here it comes!" I stiffened myself for an attack. Life has taught me that when you are ready for a blow it hardly ever comes.

One woman was spokeswoman. "You are a very clever doctor", she said, "But you are very young. We are older and we know about Kula's 'sickness'. When it attacks a woman in our villages the mother and the child die. You have saved one. You have done very well. Kula's time had come. You have no blame." Where was my stiff upper lip? It was all trembling as the tears poured down my face. Wouldn't my mother have been surprised to hear that?

And the baby? A lovely boy. Sr. Colmcille Hyland had asked me if I ever came to baptise a baby in danger of death, would I give it her name. I did; though being an ancient Irish name I thought it a strange name for an African child. It transpired that his father was a Methodist and when I explained that I had baptised the child, he was not too perturbed, but took him off to his church for further blessings and called him Jonathan. His own surname was Lahai.

Kula's mate, her husband's second wife, was brought to me for instructions on how to feed the child. She herself was childless and was enchanted with this baby. She came regularly with the child for all his childhood troubles and once I was astonished to see her breast-feeding. I admonished her about the uselessness of having the baby sucking an empty breast but she said simply: "I have milk". Disbelieving, I reached across the table and gave a gentle squeeze to what I believed was an empty breast, but instead sprayed myself in the face with milk. I sat down. For the first time I began asking questions. "How come?" I asked.

Shyly she told me that she had had a dream in which she saw Kula, who led her into the forest and showed her a certain tree. She told her that if she got the bark of that tree and stewed it, her breasts would fill. Her own mother had advised her to eat sesame seed soup. I had not until then heard of the shades of the dead assisting the living in the way just related to me. I was dismissive, disbelieving, as I felt befitted my great scientific standing, but all the same . . . thinking . . . thinking . . . Why not? Between them all they raised the child.

I was informed somewhere along the line, that the baby was confirmed and added Francis of Assisi to the medley of names bestowed on him already. (One hopes that he had a familiar Mende name as well). He is, I am told, a respected member of society in California, having done well and, as our mothers would say, made something of himself. I still hope that one day, I will meet again, Kula's son, Colmcille Jonathan Francis of Assisi Lahai.

A little laughter: The occasion for this was my first exposure to sexually transmitted disease. Not that this is in any way a laughing matter. The acute phase and implications are tragic, especially for women whose fallopian tubes block causing infertility, or possibly tubal pregnancies, which rupture and carry a very high mortality rate. What amused me was the contrast between my prudish background training, and the delightful ease with which the people I was meeting dealt with matters natural, sexual and otherwise. My entire repertoire of skills in the management of sexually transmitted diseases, as I left St. Vincent's Hospital, St. Stephen's Green, Dublin, was, as far as I remember, the number of the bus to send them somewhere else.

One day I was handed a chart with the main complaint entered as 'shortage of manpower'. "How does it affect you?" I asked. He leaned over the table and, as if imparting classified information, said: " 'Tis de woman business – dis thing no de kick" (impotence). Heavens! How was I to make things kick? Had I missed a lecture?

At that time in Sierra Leone, the prevailing sexually transmitted disease that I was able to diagnose was gonorrhoea. It is possible that contact with the outside world brought this problem, for it seems to have spread inland along the railway line. Male patients recognised this problem and came to the hospital. Women did not until it was too late.

For the first time I encountered local perceptions of disease causality and I did not understand it at all. At first I dismissed it and tried to assert my theories but later I was to learn to listen to beliefs, and ride carefully along with them. This was a problem that never went away. But to be told in the very first month, that walking over infected urine caused gonorrhoeal disease left me without anything to say that was useful. Just for a differential on causes, I was told that you could also catch it from a witch. Well!

What really brought those patients to us was either acute retention of urine or diminishing stream with severe narrowing of the urinary passage or stricture of the urethra. Was there no end, I thought miserably, to the new things that turned up? Dr. Margai came to my rescue, giving me tips and along with them courage. He dispelled the fear of mistakes in this area, with which I had been imbued as a student. The secret was to insert a catheter into the urinary passage, keep it there for several days, encourage fluid by mouth and give sulphonamides. To my amazement it worked very well. Patients would not stay in bed, which made sense given the temperatures. There was no way they would stay tethered to a bed by a urine bag. Result was they roamed around the compound in a single hospital-designed shift, ready to share their story with anyone who came.

The Mother General had come on visitation. This was an exercise in affirmation, problem-solving and in general, getting a view of the activities on the ground. A visit to the hospital was scheduled. Now the good woman in the picture had a Masters in Liberal Arts, had been novice mistress and probably came from a sheltered, rural, Irish home. She had a vague idea that medical work dealt with bodies, male and female, but little more. She encountered one of our mobile patients and asked, with becoming solicitude:

"And how are you feeling now?" "Much betta Ma." he said, lifting up his shirt and confirming his claim with appropriate visual aids.

It is probable that I had a lot of success with those cases due to all the help I got from Dr. Margai, because we were inundated with them. They sometimes turned up in agony at the convent. The convent in question at Mahei Boima Road was new and people were making a pathway, which looked like becoming a 'right of way', right past the convent front door, thus dividing our compound in two. Sister Clare took it upon herself to re-direct people taking this route. She did not like doing it and would make little tentative runs at them saying:

"Private! Private, Pa (Ma). Not here! Over yonder!"

One night about eight o'clock we returned from a trip to Pujehun, our only other convent at that time. As we came out of the car a brown, huddled shape emerged out of the velvet African night. There can be very few miseries that visit the human body, worse than that of a full bladder. It dispels fear, shame and any other emotion that has to be dispelled en route to relief. "Do Ma", the poor man pleaded, as he was being shoo-ed 'over yonder'. "Sorry for me. All dis day me no piss." Clare flew back to the convent.

The vocabulary itself was an assault. In the convent, in our training, natural functions of the body were referred to with a delicacy amounting to prudery. Indeed in some convents the sisters were obliged to take a bath with the 'chimmy' on. I rushed to the poor man's rescue, took him to the hospital and relieved his misery.

All cases did not go smoothly, of course. Sometimes the catheter came out too soon and the process had to be begun again. This was always a big disappointment for both patient and doctor.

I remember Abdul Ramiz. He was a merry faced little man from a tribe north of us. Since he was a devout Muslim, it must have been a nine days wonder to him to have us women, not only taking care of him, but in this his essential maleness. And young ones at that! I suppose our being foreigners and white explained everything. I don't know, but Pa Abdul gave us every possible co-operation, even when nothing was succeeding. He never got depressed when things did not go well, communicating his own confidence in us. "Insh Allah!" he would exclaim. Try again!

In spite of the chuckles I was often anxious. It was no laughing matter to try and restore function in these cases. Dr. Margai was my constant advisor. At one point when things were a bit difficult I decided to go away for a couple of days and see what they would look like when I got back. It is one way of dealing with a problem: leave it for a while.

I went to our convent in Pujehun where the last subject on God's earth that should emerge as table talk, was sexually transmitted diseases, so I immersed myself in proper convent conversation.

An American businessman once told me that on the first day of a cruise on the Mediterranean, he got a cable to say he had made a million dollars on the stock exchange. Well, poor man, I don't grudge him his small perks. A note was handed to me on the second day of my own vacation that read: "Relax. Abdul Ramiz can pee, straight and free."

Bo Convent: The convent in Bo was built on the old colonial lines, jalousies on all the windows, high ceilings, and verandahs all round, both upstairs and down. It was well situated in a rapidly growing Bo. Bo is the second largest city in Sierra Leone and was the capital of what, before Independence, was called The Protectorate. There were many Europeans and one winces today to recall that there was a 'European Reservation' for white people complete with club, tennis courts, swimming pool and other trappings of the 'dolce vita.' There was also an African Club and I have a feeling that it was less well endowed than that of the Europeans. It feels now like another life one lived a long time ago.

There was a large government hospital in which doctors and senior nursing staff were mainly European. Sister Concilia O'Donovan was responsible for the first primary school for girls in Bo. She had brought out a large quantity of education material from Ireland, and the school was an absolute showpiece. The children in her time went in and out of the building, with their arms folded so as not to put a mark, a single one, on the wall.

When she first arrived with two other sisters, Kevin Osborne and Felim Curley, they were accommodated in a house in Mahei Boima Road near where the present convent stands. It was given to them by the courtesy of the Demby family of Gerihun whom we remember with gratitude. The roof blew off in one of Sierra Leone's famous storms and the rain poured in, as only it can in monsoon time. The sisters then moved to the office of the boy's school as they were on holidays, and then to rooms in a place with the distinguished address of Hard Up Lane. From there, still upwardly mobile, they progressed to what is the kitchen of the present convent and finally they had a convent built.

Schoolwork, with its regular hours, was more amenable than the hospital to timetables with the strict horarium of prayer, work, meals, and recreation. If you were not present at all of the above, you were expected to make a self-accusation to the effect on your knees before the Mother Superior. Those items of the Rule became increasingly absurd, as nobody expected the doctor to leave the operating room, and sprint off to dinner or prayer exercise. These practices belonged more to the contemplative than the missionary life and it was inevitable that there would be changes.

My companion of those days was Ellen Hendrick. She was an extremely competent nurse mid-wife, a wonderful organiser and improviser, and blessed with a great sense of humour. Nuns were new on the scene in Bo so we were particularly careful about our image. We knew we were being watched and gossiped about. Would nuns see male patients? Below the belt? There had also been a sort of Kerry-man joke about a chief who asked: "If the priests and nuns did not marry, where then did the other priests and nuns come from?" We were determined not to provide any grounds for the belief that we were either the priest's wives or mistresses. We were trained to be models of religious decorum, modesty and restraint at all times, never seen where we ought not to be seen. This was not always easy. Indeed for a number of years we did not travel alone with a priest in a car. When we became better known it was no longer necessary to be so circumspect in our travel arrangements.

I am convinced that young colonial men came to consult us out of curiosity. A young man claimed that I was the only doctor in the station one day. He had an injection in the morning and that evening, on our way back from church, he came limping to the convent. The injection site was very painful, he claimed. I told him to go home and I would come and see him. "Oh law! Going to the European Reservation, and at this time of night, what will people say?", someone   moaned. We figured that we could not be too bound by the 'image' and pointed out that if we made a perfectly legitimate house call, people could say what they liked. What we did not tell anybody was that we were unable to find the house in the dark and we called at so many houses in the Reservation for directions, that the whole world knew the two young nuns were going to visit this glamorous bachelor's house. When we arrived he was in bed in dashing, striped pyjamas, hair all Brylcreemed up, making a fair double for Clark Gable in *Gone with the Wind*. A large mosquito net drooped to the ground. I got in under the net to look at the leg (which had nothing wrong with it), gave him an analgesic and was reversing out when his neighbour, another young Anglo Saxon, breezed in: "Hello Ke. . . Oh I say!"

We said good night very formally and made our retreat. We laughed the whole way home.

It was so hot. We wore so many clothes. We said Matins and Lauds at 3 p.m. I used to look at the ground and say: "One day a small pool of oil will be all that's left of me and people will say: 'That was Hilary'". Ellen and I reflected, that, although we could not shed any clothes, our hair was our own. One afternoon we went to the bathroom and not only cut off all our hair, but shaved each other's scalps. The skinheads were born. As the skull is a very bumpy place, we drew blood in a few spots with the razor. We looked like two crazy fanatics. We laughed so much that we were in no serious disposition for the evening prayer, which was about to begin. It was Ellen's turn to intone the antiphon, which that evening, happened to be drawn from Matthew: "The hairs of your head are all numbered". We both burst out laughing and the prayer session broke up. Later we prayed that we would not fall sick, and be admitted to the government hospital, looking like convicts.

Genito-urinary pathology, and with it the elephantiasis of the scrotum was new to me. Dr. Margai helped me out in these cases. The size of the utero-ovarian tumours was another mind boggler. A very young woman in those early days had a cyst that reached all the way up under her liver. When I levered it out it was attached to a simple pedicle. She was back in bed in forty-five minutes. Another case was a lipoma, growing from the shoulder reaching to the elbow. It had outgrown its blood supply, sloughed and had maggots in it. I

65

shelled it out at the shoulder under local anaesthetic, and put a few stitches in it. I don't know which of us felt the better.

For ordinary pathology I had courage enough as I had my basic degree in surgery, medicine and obstetrics. The unfamiliar on the other hand like the acute abdomen where the diagnosis was unclear, the anaesthesia of doubtful competence and the background of herbal medication unknown – all these things made it a stressful time. In fact, at the official visitation, the Mother General gave my chances of surviving in Africa a very low rating as a result of my tears over the death on the table. "Emotionally unstable" was her verdict.

I spent one year and nine months in Bo and then I was transferred to Serabu where I was to spend most of my life

7

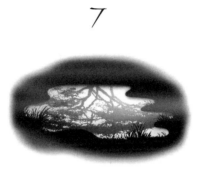

Serabu

On the seventh of October 1954, Fr. E. Kinsella C.S.Sp. drove Mother Felim Curley and me, thirty miles south of Bo to Serabu. We drove past the ferry which was situated at Bumpe, the main chiefdom town or as you might say the capital of the chiefdom. After another sixteen miles we took a right turn on to what we came to call our three-mile avenue, at the end of which we topped a hill and there lay Serabu, a small village folded into some gentle undulating hills. Houses lined the road on either side, some stretching back towards the bush, as we drove through. Up another gentle hill, through the gate on the right and we stopped right in front of the convent door. The convent was a two-story building and, as I was told, cost no more than two thousand pounds to build. Long, long ago. There was no piped water, no electricity, no telephone, no car, and no big shops. Wasn't I glad I had been raised in the country?

In front of the convent and terraced down from it stood the maternity clinic and, a little nearer and to the right, the outpatient building. At the back was a primary school. To the right, across the road, was a flat roofed cement house that, as far as I remember, was the only one of it's kind in the village at the time. Most of the houses were thatched mud and wattle, daubed smoothly and finished off with white chalk, which was plentiful in the area.

To the left of the convent ran the pathway to the parish church and the priest's residence some 400 yards away. To the left of the pathway, as far as the eye could see the rich jungle growth of Africa flourished. It was a bit spooky at night. After two days of introductions, the St. Joseph of Cluny Sisters, who were handing over this facility to us, left. Those good sisters left us all they possessed, even to the cutlery. We remember them with gratitude.

Since Serabu was not the capital of the chiefdom but one of the sections, one might ask why the Mission was founded there in the first place. One might further ask how a hospital with a very good reputation grew there. The story begins away back as many stories do. In 1898, the British imposed a tax, known historically as the 'Hut Tax'. The people rebelled, and there followed the Hut Tax War. Bumpe is reputed to have put up great resistance and, when the British got the upper hand with superior firepower, there were arrests, imprisonment, and executions. Amongst those imprisoned was Chief Makavore a native of Serabu, who was paramount chief of Bumpe. He was visited in Pademba Road Prison in Freetown by some of the Catholic Mission Priests and became interested in what they had to offer in the line of schools and other benefits for his area.

In 1904 the mission was opened in Serabu. Between 1904 and 1948, when the medical work started, two world wars had occurred. In spite of post war depression, which of course affected the colonies adversely, Frs. Joe Jackson and Harold Heard, both Spiritans, approached the Ministry of Health in Sierra Leone, and friends in Britain to make a start on health services for the people. A convent and a clinic were erected with the help of many donors, chief of whom were the Hartly sisters, Mary and Hilda, from the North of England and Mr Alex Carus who owned a cotton mill and provided surgical dressings for many years. Donor agencies as known today did not exist then.

The clinic had nine beds, a delivery room and a nursery, as well as the usual back up sluice room, toilets, etc. The babies were taken away from their mothers and placed in cots, with beautiful baby clothes, cot clothes, and a mosquito net. They were brought to their mothers for feeding. An artist-sister had done colourful murals making this an idyll in the European model. Complicated obstetrical cases were sent to Bo. This was less than idyllic as the Bumpe ferry only opened from 7 a.m. to 7 p.m. and cases had to reach there during these hours.

Serabu itself was a village of less than 2000 people and did not, during my time, exceed that figure to any great extent. Young people, having had education facilities early in the century, left the area for jobs elsewhere, thus keeping the population figures fairly stable. There were few places in the country, or indeed outside, where you would not meet a Serabu man or woman. It was a Serabu man, Matthew Ganda, who showed me how to find my way around New York many years later.

They were a farming community cultivating rice, coffee, oil palm, sweet potatoes, cassava and a great variety of vegetables, sweet peppers, egg plant, okra and lots of green leaves high in iron content, for the sauces. Christianity had been accepted but some of its tenets, particularly the marriage laws, proved difficult for the people.

So how did a hospital grow there from a nine-bed clinic? As soon as I arrived in Serabu I was obliged to set up some sort of operating facilities for reasons already mentioned. Also people followed me as if I was some new invention. Sierra Leonean medical colleagues were to tell me later that the people ascribed religious, if not magical, powers to me. Robed in white like a Muslim Haja, I lived in a house where other people did not enter, was unavailable during prayer time, and above all – and the magic of this was only told in whispers – for eight days every year never spoke a word to anyone, only prayed all day. Well, add a few spectacular lumpectomies and one can begin to understand why crowds followed me from Bo and all over the place, even from as far away as Ouagadougou in Burkina Faso.

Discarded beds from government hospitals were bought at government medical stores. Elementary operating facilities were set up. Activities went on from morning till late afternoon. Over-crowding was taken as the indication for expansion. Gradually and over the years, a surgical ward, a maternity ward and a beautiful children's ward, our pride and joy, made their appearance. Along with those there grew up a theatre, laboratory and X-Ray. A four-bed private unit was provided for those who were willing and able to pay a little extra, which went to cover costs. Eventually, a community health unit, a nurse training school and some staff quarters made the Serabu Hospital a very effective though small (120 beds) health service.

Why did we, Holy Rosary Sisters build up a hospital when the resources available to us were small to non-existent? We thought, as a result of our western training, that the hospital was the service that delivered health. We had come to provide health for the people and, with a cause like that, there must be a way. I recall a great feeling of enthusiasm, exuberance and courage. When the day's work was over and the sweat of the day washed off, letters and projects were drafted, reports drawn up, letters to individuals written, and, above all appointments made to meet with donor agencies during home leave. At least a few of these agencies must be mentioned: MISEREOR of Germany, CARITAS INTERNATIONAL of Rome – at that time I had never heard of Caritas International and actually addressed the letter to the Pope himself – CEBEMO of the Netherlands, OXFAM and CAFOD of England, APSO and CONCERN of Ireland, and a host of benefactors, some to be mentioned later. It took twenty years and more to build up the hospital, little by little, stone by stone.

Maintenance and sustainability were spectres that would rise to threaten defeat later on, but neither of these in the end, was to bring it all down round our ears. I was blessed with my companion of the early days, Sr. M. Felim Curley. There were only two of us to begin with. Gradually a Holy Rosary team was built up and there were always three to five sisters who formed the core group of Serabu hospital staff. The main bulk of the staff was composed of Sierra Leonean nationals. In time they took over from the sisters. The hospital was fortunate, over the years, to have the services of wonderful volunteers, from Ireland, Canada, the United Kingdom, Holland, Belgium and the United States. But in 1954 there were only Felim and myself. She was an amazing woman. Some 23 years my senior at the time, she played a big part in keeping me from over-work or what is today called 'burn-out', issues not in my wildest imagination at that time. She was famed for her quiet endurance of stress, physical or psychological. She was not a health professional, but had the wisdom to give priority to ensuring that the convent was a place of order, rest and prayer. This was more important than I was able to recognise at the time. But that did not stop her from coming out of the convent to help me. For the first months I did not have a professional nurse to assist me and she came to the pharmacy saying: "I can read and I can count and, if you write plain English, I can dispense tablets". And so she did.

Then one day she decided to come to the operating theatre, saying: "You never know, I may be useful in some corner some day. At least I can fetch and carry". "OK", I said. At the incision she was groping for the nearest wall to stave off a faint and I called: "Go outside, sit on a bench and put your head down ". Defeated? Not Felim. Back she came but grew faint again when she saw a tumour emerging from the abdomen. One day she gave an anaesthetic, induction with chloroform and continued with 'rag and bottle' ether. At one point she said, holding up the ether bottle: "Sister, she has had an awful lot of this". " Carry on Felim", was all I could say. Once at night, she held a kerosene lamp for me whilst I did an emergency. She stood there with arm outstretched, for I don't remember how long, but I will always remember the bugs that skid-landed on her sweat drenched arm and crawled hither and yon looking for take-off.

It was Felim who opened the first convent in Bo, with the late Sr. Kevin Osborne, and made all those exciting moves already mentioned. She opened the convent in Pujehun and later received Serabu from the St Joseph of Cluny Sisters.

I was privileged to be at her deathbed in Freetown twenty-five years later. She died quietly and peacefully, as she had lived, just as she reached her 80th year. She suffered a heart attack as she was preparing the altar for Mass and later that evening said to me: "If this is dying, it's not too bad!" The next morning, as we were speaking, she said: "Oh!" and went unconscious. In five minutes she was gone. She lies buried in the Kissy Road cemetery in Freetown in the company of the early Missionaries to Sierra Leone and beside Bishop Kelly who had invited her to Sierra Leone in the late 1940s. She was a woman to remember. I always felt her quiet presence in the Freetown convent.

'Muddah' Oliver: The Sister from whom I was privileged to take over the clinic at Serabu was Mother Oliver Cronin of the Sisters of St. Joseph of Cluny. This congregation has a long and revered history in Sierra Leone, their Mother Foundress, Blessed Ann Marie Javouhy, having visited there in 1864.

Owing to the work of those sisters in Sierra Leone, all nuns were accepted and respected as people 'about God's business', incomprehensible as their celibacy might be. St. Joseph's Sisters had already established the acceptance given to us who came later. Significantly, the local people call them 'mother', the term 'sister' never having been adopted. The local pronunciation sounds like 'Muddah', though in Krio, it is spelled 'Murdah'

I first met Mother Oliver in May 1953 at their convent in Serabu where a holiday had been arranged for me. I was not to know then that 29 years of my life would be spent in that convent. I recall those two weeks with affection. I spent my time doing illuminated lettering and listening to records, especially the tunes from 'Showboat'. There is a great poignancy in 'Ole man River' when listened to in Africa. As I basked in these idle pursuits, Mother Oliver would, every now and then, come with a problem.

She was a pint sized woman from Cork. She had preserved the lovely lilt of her county and she brimmed over with the joy of living. As far as I remember, she trained as a nurse in her more mature years and she loved looking after sick people. I have not seen, in a long life, anyone who thrived on her work as she did. Diminutive as she was, she loved a bit of excitement, and was heard to complain more than once that they had had nothing but normal deliveries for a whole month.

As a nurse/mid-wife, Mother Oliver conducted normal deliveries, ante natal, post-natal and child clinics. If, however, she ran into an obstetrical complication she had to take the case to Bo, 32 miles away, with a manually operated ferry midway. If it was at night, it was almost impossible to rouse the ferrymen. That was the time when a vehicle was shared with the parish priest. First the priest had to be located and it sometimes happened that the hapless patient delivered the baby on the way, with the priest-driver becoming an unnecessary 'extra'. The giggling group and happy mother and baby would then return to Serabu.

One day she called me to come and see a patient. He was a senior Muslim cleric with the title Alhaji. On examination he had a distended tympanic abdomen. The 'bodhrán' boys could have played on it. It was producing a selection of lugubrious growls and falsetto whines. The poor man was in agony. So we decided to admit him. He was the first man ever to be admitted in Serabu. Using local anaesthetic, I did a colostomy, intending to refer him to Bo later for diagnosis and treatment. It transpired that his problem was reversible and it was possible to close the colostomy later. Mother Oliver's excitement at this fortuitous turn of events knew no bounds. He was nursed as a textbook demonstration of perfect nursing. He was bathed, powdered and had essential foot care and toenail chiropody. Believe me, that Alhaji must have believed he had met his dream woman. A year later he came back with some other complaint and the place was full of patients. Mother Oliver had left and every body was much too busy to bother with his toenails. He took his discharge saying the place had gone to the dogs.

One night Oliver came to my room to say that she had a problem obstetrical case. She described it and I advised her to allow the patient a trial of labour until morning and if there was no progress, refer her to Bo. "The ferry is not working", she said. "In that case we will have to section her". "What do you mean?" she whispered, wide-eyed, through my mosquito net. "Caesarean section" I explained. "Jesus, Mary, and Joseph", she prayed as she fled from the room. At first light we reviewed the situation. A half dozen artery forceps, some sutures, local anaesthetic and Triline; me, two nursing aides, and Oliver was all that lay between the patient and a ruptured uterus. So we did the operation, without too much ado, except that the nurse holding the Trilene mask said at one point: "my hands are now tired holding this thing". For one frantic moment I thought she was going to leave it there, but a loaded look from me indicated that she ought to stay. She did.

Later that evening, chatting with one of the other sisters, Oliver came to tell me that our patient was doing nicely. I asked if she had passed urine and vaguely mentioned that I hoped her bladder was alright. "Oh", she said, "I'll pass a catheter". She sped away only to come back a few minutes later and coo ecstatically: "Six ounces of the loveliest urine you ever saw in your life". Poor Mother X, who had no vocation for medical affairs, sighed and said: "Thank God, I'm a teacher". The lady who had had the Caesarean always gave me a big hug whenever we met and remembered our encounter.

A year later, when St. Joseph's Sisters handed over Serabu to Holy Rosary Sisters, Oliver left with sorrow in her heart. We two would have got along just fine, but such arrangements were made way above us. I would have loved to have her but we honoured our obedience and went our separate ways.

For many years Mother Oliver ran the health centre on Bonthe Island. This was South-West of Serabu, eighteen miles by road plus four hours by launch. She sent me many patients and, whenever we met, we put our heads together about our mutual problems: running ears, tropical ulcers, protein malnutrition and so on. In those days tropical ulcers were large, painful ulcers on children's legs. They measured from one to two inches in diameter and smelled to high heaven. Dressing them to the cries of little ones was a time consuming and heart breaking exercise. There would rarely be less than ten a day. And the leg is an impossible place on which to keep a bandage. (Those ulcers were caused by an organism similar to the diphtheria bacillus and were prevented by immunisation.)

Oliver used to send me surgical and maternity cases. Like me, she always had a story. She was as agile as a spring lamb the day she told me she was 70, but not to tell anyone. She eventually retired to St. Joseph's Convent, Makeni, and there she died quietly, alone, one morning while getting ready for Mass. They found her sitting in her chair. She was in her 80's and I'm sure she did not weigh more than 98 pounds. I was in Freetown when I heard of her death and I arrived just in time for the funeral. She lies buried in the Makeni cemetery. It was sunset when we finished the last prayers. The sky was a tender turquoise and pink. An evening breeze rustled a palm tree over my head and I whispered back: "Take good care of her. She is a long way from Cork".

Getting to Know You: Gradually people began to emerge from the 'unknown' that was Serabu in 1954. There were only two of us and there we were in this small Mende village, where we knew nobody and nobody knew us. What the people felt I do not know. They were probably pleased to have acquired a doctor for the clinic and, having heard of me from Bo, they had great expectations. On my side I was anxious to have my equipment and medicines brought from Bo in order to set up out patients and surgical facilities. Secondly, and more importantly, we were to become acquainted with our local community. Those I mention here are but a few of the many who introduced us to the local scene. These encounters contributed in no small way to the subsequent development of the hospital and more significantly, to the opening up of my mind to new and other values and life styles.

There was Mama Binterabbi. Mama is a term of respect for those of mature years. White-grey then, she still lived to be a very old lady. She was a Susu by tribe, from Guinea, and spoke a smattering of Madingo and Fullah. Her knowledge of English and Mende was rudimentary. There was a small group of Fullah in Serabu and Mama had marriage connections to that group. Some were petty traders; their elders had, as in other parts of Africa, large herds of cattle. Binterabbi became a sort of hospital agent from the very outset. She had contacts in various towns across the country and in her native Guinea. The first thing I noticed was that she would arrive into the consulting room with a string of people in tow, grandly ignoring queue lines. The language situation could be hilarious. "If I can't see it and I can't feel it, I don't know what is wrong with you", I would mutter to no one in particular, as Mama stumbled, looking for appropriate words from Fullah – Susu – Mende, which the nurse turned into English for me. Mama did speculative ward rounds almost daily till her very old age, checking for patients near discharge, so that she could promise her clients an approximate date of admission. This often cut across any kind of a system we were trying to establish. When remonstrated with, she would lift her headscarf above her head showing her snow white hair, blind you with an explanatory smile and walk off. These services were probably financially rewarding, as her clientele were either in regular or diamond business.

She accumulated a mixed pot of medical information and would be convinced that treatment that worked for someone last year should be right for a totally different person this year, given that the pathology looked similar – to Mama! "This one " she would explain "is for Caesarean section right now".

Though a devout Muslim she always gave the sisters a chicken for Christmas and we gave her cooking oil for Ramadan.

Another 'agent' was Mama Wuyata. She was Mende and I

remember her clientele coming from Gbaama Konta in the east of the country. The area was rich in diamonds, so people were able to travel the distance and pay for their treatment. Wuyata always insisted that her women patients would be given a long resting period after any surgical intervention. That meant no heavy farm work, but very specifically no sex. These instructions carried a semi-religious connotation and would be observed. On occasion when these were infringed, the patient would come back to confess to me, and be re-instructed.

There were, of course, middlemen also. My favourite was 'Tee Potee See'. Sadly I have forgotten his real name. A practising herbalist in the town, he treated fevers but referred all 'lumps' to me. They were hernias, hydroceles, lumps, bumps and appendages of all sorts and once a bladder stone as big as a grapefruit. He himself, suffered from occasional urethritis. In those days a mixture of Potassium Citrate was believed to alkalinise the urine thereby making voiding less painful. He heard it called 'Mist Pot Cit' so often that he got it garbled into 'Tee Potee See', by which name he became affectionately known to the out-patient and dispensary staff.

There was Pa Karimu – Pa is a term of respect for men of mature years – who would give me advice on how to handle different situations and scold me on occasion. There was Pa Ahmadu Pessima, our only daily contact with the outside world. He had a five-ton Bedford truck and left for Bo every morning at eight o'clock, returning at three or four in the afternoon. He delegated to me all health decision-making powers for his family in his absence. No mean compliment and I treasure the memory. He once let me drive the truck a little bit and take the corner into his compound. He was scared that I would not take a wide enough swing for the corner and when I did he slapped his thigh and exclaimed: "There is a woman!" I think he was rather proud of me.

Three times a week the mail-car came, drove in the gate, stopped at the convent door where all the passengers alighted, the women making for the out patients building, while the men, with edifying decorum and believing themselves to be completely private, turned their backs to the hospital and peed into the convent flower beds. An alternative entrance was designed.

Relating to us in a different way were the members of our church. With them we worshipped and prayed. All, or mostly all, from those days are gone. Moses Sam, Pa Caulkool, Pa Keitel, Mama Titi, Mama Agatha, Mama Louisa and Mama Catherine – I can see them all wending their way up the hill to the church Sunday after Sunday.

Standing head and shoulders above them all was the late J. T. Ganda. A devout, committed Catholic he led us in prayer and singing, in discussions, in advice on what to do about various issues. Proud of his culture and his country he told me many of the Mende traditions. Strong, strict and impeccably moral, he was, in a way, Serabu.

His wife, Mrs. Louisa Ganda, affectionately known as Mama Louisa, was a delight to know. She was humorous, warm and loving. There is no other family with whom I have shared so much laughter and tears. Like everyone, they had their trials. Pa Ganda was alone in the house when Sr. Anita and I carried the news to him, at 10 p.m. one night, that his son Allie had died suddenly in Freetown.

When their youngest daughter also died in Freetown, Mama Louisa, sensing it had happened, stumbled from Marianville, her house on one hill, to ours on another hill, where we were obliged to tell her the truth. In an excess of agony she sank to the ground weeping. We joined her there and cried our fill.

We joined them also for weddings and homecomings and above all for the ordination of their son to the priesthood and later to the episcopate. There would be the carnivals of cooking and serving and dancing. The hospitality was superb.

There were, of course, in Serabu, all kinds of people as in any village: those who took advantage, those who would tell us tall stories and those who would rescue us from folly. In spite of great assistance and much advice from all quarters, I was smart enough, with the aid of Felim, to keep my own patch under my jurisdiction and fought all comers for the right to run the hospital independently.

A Tale of Three Wives: A man of those days whom I shall always remember and who influenced my life more than he was ever to know was Pa Totangie. I shall not forget him as long as I live, because for the first time I experienced an assault on my neatly wrapped Catholic beliefs. At the time I knew him Totangie was perhaps in his sixties, grey haired, a little heavy and with a pleasant, peaceful expression. He lived in a neat thatched house on the fringe of the church land, quite near the church. He had been baptised as a young man and was regular at Sunday mass. He had taught as an untrained teacher in his younger days and retired without, of course, pension or benefits. He farmed in the local bush and carried on his life and his affairs in a way that would earn him, were he in Ireland, the description of being a 'dacent respectable man' in much the same way as my father. But there, the resemblance to my father ended, for my father had to be pushed into marrying one wife when he was nearly fifty. Totangie had three.

The wife of his youth was near his own age and had two grown, educated, married, daughters. The second wife was younger, literate, and did some petty trading, especially in smoked fish, which could be collected at the Jong River eighteen miles south of Serabu. I forget where she came from or whether she had children. The third was a local woman, a small, diminutive sort of person, who, though still in her child-bearing years, had not had a child for twelve years. Secondary infertility at that point was assumed.

I liked Pa. We used to chat about lots of things, like life and its meaning, values, and traditions. Eventually the conversation came round to his polygamous situation. I was so sure that the law as I, an Irish Catholic was given it, was God's will for everyone at every time and place, that I encouraged him, kept at him, to 'fix up'. If he did, he could then receive the sacraments and go to Heaven when he died. Sic! If the law was God's will, then any ruthlessness indicated for its implementation was to be undertaken. From my island home in the North Atlantic, Catholicism was strict and disciplinary and slightly darkened by Jansenism, which, at some previous date, had filtered in amongst us. Pa listened to me and eventually decided to take action.

In the course of a year he sent his senior wife back to her family. Returning to her home in her later years, no longer productive or reproductive was an unimaginable humiliation, and added an economic burden to an already impoverished community. He had, of course, to make such financial compensation as was within his reach. Her two daughters were incensed at the disgrace imposed on their mother. There was not much they could do about this arrangement; being Catholics themselves, challenging the status quo was not then thought of.

The third and youngest of the wives he sent back to her family and the second one, the trader, he decided to marry in Church. This he did and when everything seemed settled wife number three, who had not had a child in twelve years, found herself to be pregnant. Totangie, honourable in his dilemma, came to tell me that he would pay for her ante-natal care and her delivery, and help her to raise the child, but would stay with his decision. She came to antenatal clinic. She hardly ever said anything. Her gestation proceeded normally and in due time she came into labour. The cervix dilated but she went into inertia and I was obliged do a Caesarean section. The child was perfectly normal. Post operatively she never spoke to us or to anyone who visited her. She just lay there totally inert. She did not eat. There was no haemorrhage, no infection. Two visiting doctors saw her with me. She ran no temperature. On the twelfth post-operative day she just died.

Whatever rage, humiliation or anguish tore her small heart apart we shall never know.

We had agreed that we would keep the baby at the hospital until she was one year old and able to eat adult food and she would then return to the family. But by then there was no family. The lady whom Pa had married in church turned out to be a bitter disappointment. She claimed that a wedding ring on her finger, released her from the type of obedience exacted from those in traditional marriage only. She refused to give him the profit on the fish sales and one day took all the money she could find, went 'to buy fish' and never came back.

My poor friend, victim of my zeal, retreated to a small village in the hinterland. I never saw him again. Heart broken, confused and bewildered I asked myself forlornly: "what is the Good News?" It certainly did not seem to be the rules and regulations I had come equipped with. One thing only I was convinced of as I said to myself:

"Jesus would never have done that". And neither did I ever do it again.

8

Witches and Spells

Dismissive at first of witch, swear, curse and ju-ju stories, I began to listen, and let people's faith in those things seep into me. These encounters with the vast unexplored inner spaces of people's consciousness, and of the 'otherness' in the management of human living became a sort of epiphany for me – a new light on my own faith. There are no new insights here that anthropologists do not know already. There were, however, new insights for myself.

A lady arrived in Serabu from Freetown and complained of abdominal pain of two day's duration. Freetown to Bo is 154 miles, Serabu a further 32 miles and one can imagine the discomfort of overcrowded pickup trucks in temperatures of 32 degrees or over. Her problem needed immediate surgery. This was done and an angry, inflamed appendix ready to pop, removed. I had come a long way since that first day in St. Vincent's.

There were at least a dozen excellent surgeons in Freetown, so her decision to come to Serabu was ill conceived. During convalescence I took time to sit down with her and explain about bacteria, how they can circulate in the blood, settle in the appendix, which would consequently become inflamed, perforate and put her life in danger. Surgery in Freetown would have been the decision of choice. She listened. Africans always do. But she had barely contained herself and now she burst out:

"Me, I savvy all dat bisines bout bacteria but make you tell me udat – who is that – put the bacteria in my appendix" She dismissed my explanation as missing the point altogether. She wanted to know who put the bacteria in *her* appendix.

A ready answer would not come to me. I was asking myself the age-old questions: why is one taken and one left? why her appendix and not mine or someone else's?

She took over my education.

In colourful Krio she explained: "There are wicked people in this world who acquire power to do bad to other people. You will know who they are if you are observant and listen to what they say and observe their general attitude towards you. There is a woman who owns a market stall near mine in Freetown. Many of her customers are leaving her and coming to me. She has not a pleasant way of speaking to people. She shouted at me one day, that if I continued to take her customers I would suffer some misfortune. Added to that, there is no peace at home. My husband's first wife is childless and I have four. My husband is very happy because of the children. Recently my mate has begun saying things like: "So you were in the market until this hour?"

Then my husband asks suspiciously: "Where were you?"

" Now", she concluded triumphantly "do you still think I should have attempted surgery, right there in Freetown, with those people on hand to do me a damage? "

I conceded that if witches had a range of influence, it was a good idea to move off their radar. "And how will you find out which of those two or the both of them has done this to you"?

" Oh there are ways", she said darkly.

I left it. I had enough to think about for one day.

I had learned that, in the tradition, the important question concerned *who* caused the problem not *what* caused it, the opposite to what I was teaching. The remedies I offered, like the appendicectomy in this case, worked, whatever the cause. But it seemed that the root cause of the disease lay deep in the social fabric, which, if damaged, had to be repaired. When this repair process, which could consist of prolonged rituals, came after the conventional intervention it was not so bad; but when a patient was delayed while waiting for ritual procedures, it could be disastrous for the patient, especially in maternity cases. It was the occasion of much anguish for health workers. Still the whole story and many more like it intrigued me. Was not our own Irish mythology full of stories of witches and wicked people who could work evil on the neighbours? Was I to believe such stories or not? The catechism would give them short shrift.

"I'm not pregnant": At the time when the operating facilities consisted of one set of instruments, an operating table, and an autoclave (for steam sterilising under pressure), a woman walked into the consulting room propelling in front of her the largest abdomen I had ever seen. She sat down and said: "I'm not pregnant." She said she wanted 'it' removed. She was called Mary, was aged about forty years, and had no husband and no children. Her abdomen had been growing larger for some twenty years. Her husband, believing at first that she was pregnant, was content. But when no child appeared he claimed that she had a witch. She was then put through many herbal and traditional treatments to no avail. Her husband left her; her family abandoned her. But she had guts. She sold firewood and tried for a market stall but when her abdomen continued to enlarge she was held in suspicion. If she had a witch, heaven knew what misfortune she would bring on the work place. She said: "I know my luck is here and I want it removed". I stared at it. I examined her. Except for this useless cargo she was healthy. I had read in the small print in the books that ovarian and uterine tumours could grow to enormous size and further, that their removal was not proportionate in difficulty to their size. There were historical footnotes and names of surgeons who had passed into history for removing them, in an age where the available facilities were as elementary as mine. This had been confirmed by information from our sister doctors in Nigeria.

I hesitated. I went to the books. I prayed some. I calculated the risks. Sr. Philippine Gettins, Serabu's first Matron, said: "You can do it Hilary". My decision to operate was again strengthened by the fact that I had previously operated on a very large ovarian cyst, which, as mentioned, was easy to remove. But what gave the final push was the courage and determination of this great lady. She wanted to be rid of it. She urged us to do what we could. She would play her part and the rest was left with God. She was informed in no uncertain terms that this was no easy job. She was entirely unshaken.

Preparations were made. She would have spinal anaesthetic, and maybe a kindly providence would have the tumour on a stalk or pedicle. Maybe. The main preparation was the training of a strong young man to scrub up so he could hold up this tumour while I would work my way around it and tie the blood vessels. He was called Alfred. We reckoned the thing to weigh some twenty pounds – which we figured it did but we had no scales. And I never took pictures of this kind of gross pathology. It felt it rather disrespectful.

So the day came. A long incision extending the whole length of the very stretched abdomen and this mountain of fibro-myoma reared up in front of me. Alas! It was not going to be one of the easy ones. This was going to take courage and speed – and the strength of Alfred. For one thing, the spinal only gives at most an hour and a half. For another thing, there was no blood bank so you simply did not spill blood. And there was no going back. It is not possible in a tumour of this size to close up and declare it inoperable. And I had not counted on the leash of blood vessels from other organs that fed the tumour. But there was no way back. "Hold it up Alfred!" "Don't weaken Alfred!"

I cheered myself on by reminding myself that after all this is not a vital organ; once out, she won't miss it. You could say that again. And these blood vessels are not the superior thyroid or renal arteries, so dissect gently, cut, tie. And at last it is in a medium sized oval bath on the floor, filling it to capacity. Sewing up – "Alfred, you may go" – then back to bed.

It was a long and difficult post-op. She developed some predictable complications but recovered. Her abdominal muscles were paper-thin and we were obliged to procure a corset for her. The corsets of the time had whale- bones in them and would, we hoped, restore some shape to her body. She was eventually discharged and went back to Freetown where she lived.

I often think of her. Did she migrate to Freetown or was she born there? The name Mary would suggest a Christian background; did she go to school? What dreams of her girlhood had vanished? I forget these things now but am not likely ever to forget her indomitable spirit, as during that gruesome surgery she sang quietly, in a wavering, tuneless voice, perhaps to encourage us: "Dancing with my shadow, feeling kind of blue; Dancing with my shadow making believe it's you."

Sista! Sista!: I was not very long in Serabu when a young Lebanese man from the next village appeared under my window at 11 p.m. at night.

" Sista! Sista! Good evening Sista ! Sista!"

He had disdained the use of the clamp and string (the string had a clamp at one end and a bell at the other beside my bed), confident that direct negotiation would prove more effective. I leaned over the window, an unlikely Juliet and asked: "What is wrong? What is it?"

"My boy's wife is seriously ill in the village and I want you to come and see her. I have my truck here, Ah go pay" (I will pay).

" Where is the place?"

" Taninahun"

Taninahun! Saints preserve me! Nine miles from Serabu. What did he think I could do in a dark house in the night when the facilities were so meagre where I was? Added to that he was annoying me standing there with his two hands in his pockets, shifting his weight from one side to the other trying to be nonchalant. "Ah go pay" being the answer to everything.

" Bring the woman in here", I called down to him.

" Her head is turning and she cannot stand", he persisted.

" Bring – her – in", I spelled out and went back to bed muttering to myself that more than one head is turning.

He brought her the following morning. I diagnosed a ruptured tubal pregnancy of two days duration. I had never actually seen one before, except in the books. The ferry at Bumpe was not working, so I decided to operate. Induction with chloroform maintained on 'rag and bottle' ether. She was a big, strong woman and it took an amount of ether to keep her down. I was, myself, all boozed up by the time we finished.

As I nicked the peritoneum, blood oozed out like lava, pouring down the side of the table, down my gown, all over the place, an unholy bloody mess. There were no transfusion facilities and no suction. The idea of auto-transfusion had not yet come to me. Later we became expert at auto-transfusion. The blood collecting bottles were autoclaved and placed on the instrument tray. As soon as a nick was made in the peritoneum, a small stainless steel jug was used to collect the blood. It was poured through gauze into a blood-collecting bottle, and as soon as full, popped back through a vein, which was kept open for the purpose. These cases did so well. Sometimes the abdominal cavity would yield three units of blood. We never washed out the peritoneum or went to the trouble to remove clots. The immediate objective was to reverse the shock, tie off that fallopian tube and send her back to bed. That I did.

"That was fast", said my only trained nurse in awe.

All evening I waited, my heart in my mouth. It was the time that high tech had just hit Serabu in the form of what was then called a gramophone. The proud owner had returned from Nigeria, a retired railroad official, and it was of the essence that this piece of equipment would be heard as far away as possible. The only problem was, that at that time, he had acquired only one record. It was "Ole Faithful".

"Ole Faithful, we roam the Range together" stole across the still dark nights and enveloped us like our mosquito nets. We woke up, probably and appropriately, to "hurry up Ole fellow. . ." The afternoon of the operation however, Ole Faithful grated on my anxiety. When I saw the nurse approach I asked urgently: "Yes! What is it? Yes?" As coolly as if we were discussing pumpkins she said: "That patient's drip is getting finished". Whew! She made a splendid recovery, as I was to learn later that such cases do. It took more out of me than it did out of her.

But the episode had a sequel. The Lebanese man who brought her belonged to a family living in a chiefdom headquarters town nearby.

The Lebanese came early in the century to Sierra Leone, and were, as has been said, great traders – almost from Syro-Phoenician times. They were mainly traders in produce, which was brought from other parts of the country to the capital, Freetown, in their trucks. They returned with imported goods: clothes, tea, sugar, tobacco, kerosene, cheap jewellery, bales of cloth and anything and everything that a farmer would need and buy when he sold his produce. Many were also in the import and export business.

My friend of the window scene had money and was flamboyant about it.

" No worry for money, Sista. Ah go pay", he urged me the next day, implying that I probably could do better if a little further oil was applied.

" I will give you the bill later" I promised and meant it.

" Well! look money for the Church, Sista".

"Thanks" I said and added quickly: "The hospital is different. You will still be given a bill for the patient".

He once more provided the magic formula: " Ah go pay".

"You go 'gree admit her for upstair for convent?" he now ventured.

Good gracious! We had enclosure at that time and no one, cleric or lay, was allowed in the area where our bedrooms, community and dining rooms were, so I was obliged to disabuse him of that idea straight away.

I began to wonder what the source of this quite extraordinary altruism or charity was. It turned out that she was not his boy's wife at all but his own mistress. She was also another man's wife and he had been obliged to flee with her to a village away from the wrath of her husband who was none other than the Paramount Chief.

A vain man with money! I explained to him that I needed more equipment and, playing shamelessly on his vanity, I described how he might have his name inscribed on, for example, a new instrument trolley for the theatre. He liked the idea and did help. Other items followed. He bought us our very first generator. It was only 3KVA and Anita and I could crank it up. We learned to recognise air lock and bleed the system, but we were not really great mechanics and nearly had the hands burned off us as our job moved us between dettol and diesel.

It was with great sorrow that we watched our friend take too many chances: gambling, wine, women and money. He did a spell in prison before he died in great need. I have retained a soft spot for him in my heart. He was a happy 'devil may care' sort of person for whom life might have gone the other way.

May his better self be at peace.

"More to Life . . ." Musaila was about forty-five years old and a native of a village not far from our hospital when I first came to know him. For a man, he was slightly built and what they would call in the west of Ireland, 'hardy'. He had an expressive smile. It could be glad, rueful or sympathetic, but what was special to himself was his eyes. African eyes are usually brown and soulful, like still dark pools, but Musaila's eyes danced. They were the liveliest, merriest brown eyes I have ever seen.

There was an extraordinary contentment about him. He had been sick and had no money to pay the bill so he asked to stay on and work in lieu. He cut grass with a machete, fetched and carried and was so suitable in every way that he was kept on. He rented a little room in a house in the village, came and went and did his work. He liked what he did, took an interest in affairs general and particular around the place.

A good worker, faithful and loyal, he would come forward if we foreigners needed a bit of advice. If he recommended another worker, you could be sure he also was reliable.

As time went on, he expressed the wish to become a Christian. He just wanted to belong. In his forthright, honest way he counted the cost, the implications. It was explained to him that a Christian was expected to love God and show it by worship; to love his neighbour and show it by love, honesty, truth, and marital fidelity. Most of these things presented no great problem to Musaila. The crux was church marriage. It is possible that he had had a wife in earlier life who had either died or left him. The Church requires that marriage vows be exchanged in the presence of a priest, the civil register being signed at the same time. This poses a serious problem to traditional people.

What this means is that western style laws governing the marriage contract are imposed on the couple. According to these, the woman may inherit property and may contest custody of the children, to mention but two such laws. In the traditional way marriage is arranged between families, supported throughout by the families, and dissolved by the families. Arrangements are also made by the families to support the children, should this become necessary, and to support the woman until she finds another husband. A husband is the normal social security for the woman. The differences between traditional marriage and marriage in church are administered respectively by the national government administration and the native law and the custom of ages. Added to facing a church marriage, which Musaila's family would advise him against with all their might, he wished to find a girl who was a Christian, or willing to become one, and who would say yes.

So the search began. One day, his eyes alive with mirth, he came to tell me that his family had found a girl for him with four years secondary school education.

"How you see such a thing", he chuckled: "Me no savvy book and me wife savvy plenty". (I illiterate and my wife literate). He was not arrogant but a realist. This would not work out in the social structures of the day. I laughed myself as I said:

"For true, Musaila, dis no go work."

The search went on. One day he brought a nice young girl of about twenty years of age: "This is Bendu. The families don 'gree sey mek we marry" (The families have agreed to our marriage). My western self shot back: "Bendu eself don 'gree?" He allowed her to answer. She smiled shyly and said yes.

He wanted her admitted to the convent boarding school where she would learn some housekeeping and take her instruction. She took the name Margaret at baptism some six months later. We saw to it that she retained her lovely Mende name as well. They were married and were happy as we expected they would be. Margaret became pregnant almost at once. Their son was called Augustine.

Musaila had no land and no resources, other than a paltry labourer's wage, which would not exceed twenty dollars a month. It was reminiscent of rural Ireland in the 1930's. People married then and raised large families with great courage, always believing that if God gave children, he would take care of them. Their God was real, a providing God. So it was with Musaila.

About this time it was noticed that he was losing weight and his work started to go off. I spoke to him sharply and raised my voice. Musaila lifted a gentle prohibitive hand and said:

"Le we keep dis compin tok" (talk between friends). I came down an octave and felt chastened. I discovered that he had been having repeated urinary tract infections, and had been receiving treatment at the outpatients. I examined him and found he had a large mass in his lower abdomen. "Please God", I prayed, as I made the incision, "let this be removable". In previous patients I had removed a bladder stone and a prostate, both of which were palpable in the lower abdomen like a three months pregnancy. So I was hopeful, but also doubtful. Poor Musaila had no such doubts. He had seen all sorts of pathology come to surgery and go home. I think he believed I could cure anything.

As I exposed the tumour tears sprang to my eyes. It was clearly malignant, the result of long standing Bilharzia. Poor Musaila, poor Margaret, poor little Augustine.

After the surgery, when the pain had subsided, Musaila was able to identify that the tumour was still there.

He asked me at rounds: "What does this mean?"

Holding his once merry eyes, now grave and steady, I said quietly: "Musaila, that lump is growing there and cannot be removed." He only said: "Oh" and looked away into the distance for some moments. " Call George" he said. George, his brother who was outside, came in. Musaila placed him on one side of the bed and me on the other and addressed us both:

"Make sure that, in time, Margaret marries a Christian husband and see that Augustine is sent to school and raised Christian."

We promised. He was content. I wandered away from the bed humbled and graced. He had nothing you might say and at the last bridge, which we all have to cross, he had everything. I was reminded of the words of Maurice Sindak: "There must be more to life than having everything."

He went down hill steadily and died quietly some months later. The place was not quite the same without him. I hope he is praying for us till we all meet right merrily in Heaven.

Margaret, in time, married a Christian and raised a fine family, but that is another story.

As for Augustine, he did go to school and was raised a christian. He told me recently that his young wife died in child-birth in a sickle-cell crisis. Dear Lord does the road wind up-hill all the way?

Ain't No Such Thing! Bockari W. was a small man, about five feet tall or less, and when first seen he was carrying a grotesque scrotal mass hanging down almost to his ankles. Walking for Bockari was a big hazard. His was not the biggest ever seen. Recourse to a wheelbarrow to move around has been reported.

The condition is caused by a tiny organism called Filaria Bancrofti, that blocks the lymphatic drainage system and causes, sometimes, gross swellings in the extremities, mostly the legs or scrotum. The local people believe that, such conditions are caused by breaking taboos. The psycho-social effect of a scrotal swelling of this dimension is disastrous. The unfortunate victims are always destitute unless supported by a very special family, but more often they are ostracised. Bockari was reasonably well nourished so he was one of the lucky ones.

Understandably he did not come through the consulting waiting room. Moving along a queue was not his favourite activity. He waylaid me round a corner where he would be less noticeable. He was leaning forward on a stick, his long cotton gown doing little to hide the diagnosis. He was short by any standard but leaning forward he looked even shorter. Coming straight to the point, he looked up at me and said: "I have come"! "So I see", said I "For the operation" he explained as if we had already discussed it or I had had some notice of his coming. I had never seen him before.

It was late afternoon and it had been a long day, I was hungry and bone tired and in my heart I was saying: " I do not want ever to do one of those operations again."

The job is messy, the skin preparation of such a huge mass of wrinkled and often verucous skin is almost impossible. Post operative infection is common in our conditions, handling a tumour of that dimension is back breaking and, of course, such people are outcasts and never have a penny to contribute to the expenses.

"You have come for surgery?" I asked.

"Yes". He leaned a bit heavier on the stick as if drawing strength up out of the ground. We stood there, confronting each other, I weakly determined that this one would go to the government hospital, and he strongly determined that I would be his surgeon. "How about going to the government hospital in Bo?" I suggested.

He looked at me earnestly and then carefully: "I want you to do my operation because you are a God person"

I had long since suspected that people who said these things to me were not seeing a halo around my head. They probably had been to the fortune-teller who would have told them where their luck was. It is certain that Bockari knew I knew this. Having played our little game I turned to the nurse who was chuckling, because it was not the first time she saw me give way in face of a stronger force. "Admit him, check out his general condition and put him on the list for next week".

In the event there was nothing spectacular about Bockari's surgery but as I walked back to the convent my mind wandered back to the first one I ever saw.

It first came to my notice in a small inset, in small print, at the bottom of a page of Romanis and Mitchner, a textbook in use for final medical year. I passed the book across to Sr. Lucy in the study and she wrote: "There ain't no such thing. Couldn't be". I felt better. But it was waiting for me in 1953 when I was new in Bo. One day, Ellen Hendrick, who was the nurse with me at the time, came into the consulting room, eyes wide: "My God", she said, "Come and see". I did. The poor man was sitting on a bench with one leg on the ground, the other and the huge scrotum on the bench, as it were, beside him. Joseph, the only male nurse in the small place, was anxious for me to be surgically courageous. I had courage enough for anything I had been taught to do, but this! "Spare me", I pleaded.

Joseph brushed aside my anxiety. "You think it's difficult because you are not seeing it in your country. I have done so many with Doctor (Margai), I can direct you".

We gave a spinal and Joseph directed: "Make a vertical incision extending from 'here to here', and now incise a circle which will be the base to attach the penis". "If we ever see it" I interrupted. Joseph ignored me. "Insert a tissue forceps along this tunnel" he said, indicating a sort of scrotal belly button, "grasp the tip of the penis and draw it down". Having done this and got a place for it, I wrapped it in a moist sponge. Next the testicles were isolated, similarly wrapped and folded over the groin. If Joseph knew Percy French he would have said: "All the way home is down hill". And so it was. Blood vessels were easy enough to pick up. They were silhouetted in the transparent blubber of grossly oedematous tissue. Lymphatic fluid poured all over the place, down the table and down our gowns. It took about five blades to incise the huge area of skin which had toughened over the years. Such was my introduction to elephantiasis of the scrotum. I did many over the years and, after each one, I would vow never to do another. We often had problems with the final design. When the patient's condition was good, blood pressure stable, the spinal anaesthetic still working, a little jocularity would surface as we tried to restore some aesthesis in the area. We sometimes fetched up with a tubular model, a triangular one, or one with a 'lug' where it never ought to be.

There was nothing spectacular about Pa Bockari's surgery, but there was something special about himself, which is why I remember him so well from all of the others. Like Sam McGee, "He wore a smile you could see a mile". He had a small face, slightly prominent teeth, but very white. He always wore a cap with a top tassel on it which, with his small urchin face, made him not unlike a leprechaun. When he discovered the improvement in his nether anatomy, his smile lit up the ward. He switched on that smile, as Sr. Eileen used to say, like a light on Broadway, and sent us into gales of laughter. Actually, he never left us. He took a job as a porter and could be seen carrying trays from the kitchen until his death from a heart condition some years later.

He made his small contribution, but his greatest gift was the smile he left to glow across the years and gladden us.

"Do your best.": It was a public holiday and everyone had as much off duty as could be managed. I was basking in the hope of no great problems in the course of the day. It was not to be. The nurse said that a baby had been brought in to the children's ward and needed my attention right away. The parents were from a nearby village and had waited, hoping, that the child would improve. In answer to my question "what is the trouble?" they unwrapped a one-month old child that weighed two and a half kilos. A large tumour about the size of an orange had pushed its way upwards in the appendix area. It looked mountainous in the tiny little abdomen. The child was alert but as emaciated as a famine victim. The family had tried herbal medicines and now, they said, would I please operate and remove 'this thing'. I could not prevail on the family to seek more expert skill than I believed myself able to provide. I explained, what they already knew, that the child had a very precarious hold on life, and confessed that I had never seen such a large tumour in such a small child before. As usual, they said: "Do your best; the outcome is left with God". I looked up the books hoping to find some information on this condition but there was nothing in the books available to me. Fortunately I had the assistance of Mary Maher, a paediatrician, and we decided to do what we could. We took him to theatre, and, as he was hypo-thermic, placed his tiny little body on a hot water bottle on the operating table. The child looked so small and defenceless on the large table that it took the courage of both Mary and me to proceed. Mary sedated him and I gave a small dose of local anaesthetic. Carefully, slowly, I incised paper-thin skin, and exposed the sparse strands of underlying muscular tissues. As I attempted to separate these strands – pop! Pus gushed out. I placed a drainage tube in what was clearly an abscess and sent the baby back to bed. Mary took care of the post-operative period. I was surprised one day to find her giggling to her self at his bed-side. "I was just thinking", she said, " if this were back in St. Christopher's, Philadelphia (where she trained), what a team would be at work: consultant paediatricians, special nursing staff and round the clock intensive-care. Now look at him!" He smiled forty-eight hours later. A smile is a child's way of saying: "All is well with me". Episodes like that made any day a great one.

Our little patient made remarkable progress and became a regular visitor at the under fives clinic, where his mother showed him off and told the story over and over.

9

Never a Dull Day

One would like to describe a normal day but there was no such thing. There was the regular convent routine such as the time of rising, the time of prayer and mealtimes and one tried to hit them as best one could. 'As best you could' became acceptable as the years went by. Profound silence and fasting from midnight lasted a long time.

The emergencies nearly always came at night – fear comes with the dark. The commonest were Caesarean section for ante partum haemorrhage or ruptured uterus; strangulated hernia and ruptured tubal pregnancy were also common. They were real nightmares. The generators could fail, and sometimes did, no really proper anaesthesia, no blood bank and, for the first fifteen years, I was the only doctor. Three Caesarean sections in one night, or an acute abdomen with some weird pathology and it was a very sleepy, thirsty body, who was barely present at the 6.30 Mass the next morning.

I have a few heart-stopping memories of generator failures at the wrong moment. One night the generator stopped just as I was incising the lower segment in a Caesarean section. The patient had had a spinal anaesthetic and was perfectly conscious. Quickly but calmly I reassured her, explaining that this part of the operation could wait a little and not to worry.

"There is a good lamp in my room if you would like to send for it", offered the patient calmly.

And there was a morning when we woke up to find, that the victim of a road transport accident of the previous night, had bled into his chest, was in shock and once more the power had failed. My heart misses a beat as I remember it. The maintenance man restored the power in time and Lucy and I saved the patient. Ironically he was an American who had come safely through Vietnam, only to come near to death on a quiet road in Africa.

We lost some patients, of course, but we never lost anyone for want of light, as far as I can remember. There was always a lamp.

As well as the medical hazards, there were the usual tasks which keep a place going and growing: generator and building maintenance, staff management, the night hours stolen from sleep for correspondence and administration.

How, one may ask does the lone doctor survive?

Youth, physical strength, health, a hobby and a sense of humour are pre-requisites. Youth is a big bonus only it is something that does not keep. The Mendes have a great sense of humour and can laugh when there was often little enough to laugh at. And they are splendid mimics. I have seen myself as others see me more than once.

On the practical side, doctors and qualified nursing staff trained and delegated skills down along the nursing ranks. I cannot remember when I lost the skill of finding a scalp vein in a baby – lost it, that is, to nursing aides. They became adept at some diagnoses. Sometimes a note would reach me at night via clamp and string: "They have brought wan woman she have ruptured his uterus we have call theatre come." Never mind the English. That would be the job of a registrar in Ireland. Of course it is true that the further down the ranks one distributes skilled tasks, the greater must be the supervision. What you gain on the swings . . .

In many parts of Africa theatre nurses become so expert, after long years as assistant to the surgeon, that they operate on hernias, hydroceles, and appendicitis with great success. I met an English doctor who, working alone in a large Mission Hospital, developed an acute appendicitis and had surgery by the assistant nurse. Humbling. But it makes a lot of sense in the vast road-less territories of Africa and Asia.

The indispensable aid to the survival of the lone doctor in my experience is the nursing staff, religious, volunteer and national. They taught, they trained, they improvised from nothing, and they took night calls either with us or instead of us, where possible. Together we battled through horrific nocturnal dramas and daylight travels. When things went well we had the 'craic.' In surgery, patients always wanted to see what had been removed. Bob O'Connell used to say that you should never operate for gallstones without a few in your pocket!

In later years the convent routine changed out of recognition as we began to spend days and/or nights in the villages, conducting under-five clinics, training programmes, various campaigns and discussions. Curiously, adjustment to a less structured day was not immediately liberating for me. I had come to believe that the rule, the silence, regularity and uniformity constituted a 'better way'. When a hospital call coincided with the time for Matins or Vespers I answered the hospital call, later wondering if I should say the prayers unavoidably omitted, perhaps staying up late to do so. Once more I was being drawn in opposite directions, experiencing the dualism of sacred versus secular. Gradually I learned, and continue to learn, a balance between prayer, work and leisure that gives true freedom of spirit.

For me, times spent in the villages were unforgettably happy, though I cannot deny the discomfort of the heat and the lack of sanitation. We were well fed, and marvelled at the hospitality of the people. I had thought hospitality was a Christian virtue but found that it is, of course, highly prized by Islam and equally so by those who belong to neither of these two traditions. These experiences continued to expand my consciousness and forced me to seek for the richness of spirit in all people that lies deeper, and is more universal, than all religions.

Travel in the Fifties: Within Sierra Leone our travelling would have been mostly to Bo, Freetown or Pujehun. Bo was a good shopping centre, boasting a railway station and many firms that were collecting and exporting produce to their respective countries. There was the British G. B. Olivant at Bo (GBO), the Greek Patterson Zocchonis (P.Z.), the French Compagnie Francaise de L'Afrique Occidental (CFAO), and Uniliver's United Africa Company (UAC). Also, and importantly, there was the Swiss Cold Storage Company, which imported food for the colonial population and anyone else, including missionaries, who cared to or could afford to buy them.

Serabu/Bo was the usual excursion. It was undertaken by lorry with the dependable Mr. Ahmadu Pessima. Some took their own chairs in the back of the truck or up front if the seat was available. 'Pa Pessima', as he became familiarly known to us, gave untold service to the hospital in those days, carrying letters, groceries, building materials and ourselves. The petty dishonesty of later years was rare then. Pa brought the goods and the change without a problem.

Trips to Freetown (160 miles) were few. The road in 1953 and '54 was through Danballa, Mongheri, Kumarabi and on to Mile 91 and thence to Freetown. The roads were laterite, the best of them running on hard upland surfaces, where the gravel gathered in the centre, leaving the sump vulnerable to damage. Some parts turned into huge wash-board-like surfaces which made control of the vehicle tricky. Did one fare better by tearing over them or going slowly? In other places where the road ran in swampy areas, there were potholes. When the rains came this changed for the worse. Potholes deepened, road bases sank, and swampy areas became churned up into a sludge that sent vehicles down to the axle. Some roads became impassable for a few weeks every year.

At that time only the last twenty miles to Freetown were tarred. Gradually bridges were constructed, and new roads made. Sadly, as with all new things, many villages were by-passed and their economy suffered. One change gave Serabu a nine-mile short cut off the main road into the hospital. It has been said, however, that when new recruits arrived and turned off the main road, through Taninahun to Serabu, the stoutest hearts quailed. People were known to mutter: "My God, will I ever get out of this place?" The reason for this was that so lush is the growth of the forest/bush during the rains, that at most times of the year there is a wall of near twenty feet of dust-stained growth on either side where monkeys frolicked with great grace. Ten or fifteen miles of this gave the impression of penetrating to the point of no return.

Ferries were a special feature of travel in the fifties and well into the seventies. These were moderately safe if the rivers were not running in spate during the monsoons, but for new arrivals they were quite daunting. Two ramps led up to a float. Sometimes the ramps did not reach the bank, or they were in poor repair, so that driving on or off the ferry demanded skill and daring. The ferryman stood on the centre of the float and called out directions. At the beginning these were more mystifying than helpful: "hut am . . ." the rest of the sentence would be acted out charade wise indicating 'right', 'left' or 'straighten out'. Once the car climbed on board the float, the ramps were drawn up and the conveyance drawn manually across the river, using a stout cable attached at the other side. A letter home describing this, drew my father's only admonition: "Don't drown for goodness' sake", he pleaded, "die for the faith if you must, but as for plain drowning, you could have done that at home". One feature of the ferries was that in the rainy season they could be closed if the river rose beyond a certain level. Ferrymen were strict and you could cross a raging current in a dugout canoe if you had the courage, or you could stay wrong side of the river until the rains abated; ferrymen would not budge. The ferry at Bumpe separated us from the nearest referral hospital at Bo, which was often a problem for us. Delays were common. Six to eight trucks could be lined up at a ferry, especially on the Freetown road. If the hapless passenger was at the end of the queue and it came to 7 p.m. when the ferry closed, he could sleep there. This had an effect on people's driving. For ten miles before a ferry no vehicle ever 'gave road'. The rush was for the ferry. Travelling on laterite roads in the wake of another vehicle, rushing in order to reach the ferry before closing time, mantled everyone in red, laterite glory.

On one occasion in August 1954 we went on a visit to Pujehun, our only other convent at the time. That convent was an old mission house built in red burned brick. One of its claims to fame was that Graham Greene is said to have written part of *The Heart of the Matter* on the veranda upstairs. Scobie probably was born of his fertile imagination there. In Pujehun he needed little imagination to describe, as he did so powerfully, the monsoon rains, the humidity, the sweat – and the vultures.

On that trip we crossed the ferry at Sewa, the bigger of the three rivers to be crossed, the other two being Bandajuma and Yaweh. I was driving and negotiated the three ferries without too much trouble. On the return journey we found the Sewa ferry closed because rain having continued all day, the river had risen beyond the prohibited level. We were only six miles from home and the day was drawing to a close. We turned quickly and covered the 42 miles and two ferries to Pujehun, where we spent the night. We tried again the following day but were blocked again at Sewa. The only option now, was to drive to Kenema, and put the car and ourselves on the train.

Kenema was a further 48 miles of rain-damaged road. Heavy wind and rain had hurled charred branches of trees across the road at several places. These I was obliged to drag out of the way. White robes now well blackened from my exertions, I presented myself to the stationmaster at Kenema railway station. Between us, we had not enough money for the car and ourselves, and to our embarrassment we heard the stationmaster asking Bo for advice.

The telephone appliance consisted of the old two-piece on the wall. He bellowed into it: "There are Roman Catholic Sisters here. They have not got sufficient money to travel. Advise. Advise."

Bless my soul! Vow of poverty we might have but who wanted it to show? A policeman from Bo at once stepped forward and gave us the money. The stationmaster then presented me with another problem. Would I please have the vehicle 'chocked' I asked: "What? Who? Where? How?" in rapid succession. Someone directed me to the Public Works Department. Breathless, I burst into an office where two Europeans sat, and implored them to come and 'Scotch' the vehicle, or the train would leave, and we knew no one in Kenema. As soon as the man spoke I knew he was Scottish and that I had used the wrong word. I drove the car on to the float and the Public Works Department carpenter came, put security wooden blocks at the front and back wheels and we took off. At Bo I was to reverse the car off the float but now, after negotiating seven ferries in 48 hours, I was tired, wet, dirty and hungry, and my nerve failed. "Sista don 'fraid?" someone laughed. "Yes", I agreed "Sista 'fraid bad now; please take the vehicle off for me." They did. That night I dreamed I was driving up a wall and was having problems with the windows.

The railway ran from Freetown to Pendembu. Not noted for speed or punctuality, the railway was later closed down, mainly because it was running at a loss and the gauge was too narrow to connect up with neighbouring countries, a development which might have made it financially viable. The closure was a pity I think because the railway carried much freight as well as passengers. Even though it was often late, frequently de-railed, and unbearably hot to travel in, the train was always there, and did arrive eventually without tearing up the roads as the trucks were to do later.

Up to the late 1960s travel to Europe by mail boat was common. Letters from Europe by boat took two weeks and, as the inland service then was pretty good, it was a satisfactory service. Boats anchored out in the harbour before the Queen Elizabeth II Quay was built. Passengers were lowered on to waiting boats and taken ashore. On my first trip home in 1957, I clambered up the side of a cargo ship on a rope ladder, my dress, scapular and veil flying all over the place. I must have looked like a large dismembered bird against the side of the ship.

Later when crossing rivers I was to learn to be comfortable in boats that, even with an outboard engine, were of doubtful nautical competence. Sometimes the engine would fail and we would drift, cruising quietly down the river, going nowhere that I could see, until the boatman would get the engine going again.

I never learned to relax in a 'dug-out' canoe, even though it is the loveliest way of river travel, perfectly noiseless in dream-like scenery, but the barque is fragile, the space confined and the boat man always says: "just sit and do not move", which is not very re-assuring. Once I asked the young boy who was dreamily paddling the canoe with the end of a banana leaf, if the big fish that eats people was ever seen in this river. "Plenty", he said. "Thanks a ghrá" I said, "you've made my day".

Trip to Remember: Enter the sixties and Sierra Leone Independence. The economy was promising. Everything, we believed, was getting better and better. The world and we were young. Lebanese handled most of the commercial sector. They bought and sold palm kernel, coffee and at one time, rice. They brought back from Freetown marketable products for their shops, which were choc-a-bloc with everything from a needle to an anchor.

The big ambition for young Lebanese men was to own a Mercedes Benz. These they drove luxuriously fast and as ostentatiously as possible, when and wherever roads permitted. Given that all roads, even those well surfaced, were exposed to the incursion of goats, chickens, or children, this was a dangerous exercise. We occasionally got lifts to Freetown in these marvellous cars. One such a trip is unforgettable.

Farid was about eighteen years old. He had been sent to Lebanon for his education and now recalled to a rural area to join in the family's business. It was a comfortless situation with mediocre accommodation and he was bored. Any excuse for a trip to the capital would do. I was one. His mother, a devout Muslim, with many family health problems, would do anything for 'Sista'. So off we went. I watched the speedometer mount from 55 to 60 – 65 – 70. And this, with one elbow out the window, the other hand lightly on the steering.

On the seat between us was a selection of small records. In the dashboard, where nowadays the radio and tape recorder are located, was a record player. I had not seen its like before nor have I since. Farid briefly removed his one controlling hand from the steering, to give the records a shuffle and ask me what I would like to hear. "Oh," I said eagerly, "Farid, why don't you do the driving and I'll do the disc jockey." I was hoping that a soothing record would steady the pace. As the needle tipped seventy-five miles an hour, I picked up a record. It happened to be Jim Reeves singing: "Precious Lord Lead Me Home"! "Oh Lord", I silently prayed, "Do just that, for I'm coming now for sure and at seventy five miles an hour". "And, dear Lord", I added, "Could you also be ready to receive a couple of goats and chickens, for I see some of them do not know about us bearing down on them at seventy five miles an hour". I turned the record. The flip side was, "This World is not my home, I'm just a passin' through. If Heaven's not my home, then lord what shall I do?" I played these two for the whole four hours to Freetown. "Sister likes Jim Reeves", Farid marvelled to himself.

The particular town in which Farid lived drew its prosperity from the railway and the main road to Freetown which passed through there. It was then a bustling small town, perhaps better called a trading post. Five-ton trucks were either loading up produce for Freetown, unloading things for the shops or dealing with the railed materials. The shops stocked kerosene, bush lamps, candles, sugar, tea, corn flour, cigarettes, sweets and later chewing gum. Fancy nylon underwear was always draped ostentatiously for the men to buy for their wives, chief among which were heavily padded bras called 'cock bobbi'. Bobbi is the Krio word for breast, while cock indicates the purpose of the garment.

When the railway closed and the road by-passed the town it's prosperity died out. Of seven Lebanese shops that I can see in my mind's eye, not one remains. Shutters closed, they look blindly out on the street, silent witnesses to an era swept away.

Life without T.V. People often asked how we entertained ourselves. We made our own fun and some was made for us. Given that a journey of forty-eight miles could turn into a saga of epic proportions and that everyone involved would have their own rendering, there was a lot of in-house humour and stories. The hospital, the village, the work, and always seeking new ways to do more and do it better, made the life stimulating.

In African village life, there are a great number of celebrations. Births, deaths, marriages and initiations are celebrated in dance, food, wine and song. Africa celebrates life, no matter how tenuous the thread that holds it. Nothing, neither poverty, sickness, nor the hard road to a better life, with all its ups and downs, can extinguish the spirit of celebration in Africa. Sunday liturgy is spontaneous, original, and exuberant. People love to sing. There is a choir but people join in with gusto. The offertory procession can have a long line of gifts for the support of the priest: potatoes, yams, pumpkin, beans, chickens and money. All gifts are brought to the altar in dance to the accompaniment of drums, 'shake-shake' and other local instruments.

On Sundays and great celebrations the crowds are large and at the sign of peace, there is a Mardi Gras of everyone reaching as many friends as possible, to smile, hug or shake hands. Sometimes too long and sometimes too loud, but who cares? Liturgy is the celebration that it is meant to be.

Spontaneous prayer is really spontaneous, like: "Oh Lord! it is true what the priest has said. We like revenge. It is very bad and we pray you to deliver us from it but hope you will take revenge for us yourself at the tail end". Or one Good Friday: "Let us pray for the repose of the soul of Our Lord Jesus Christ".

People take the trouble to dress for Church. Women, in particular, can make headdresses, using yards of coloured material that would put designers right out of business. Differing from their sisters in the West, African women, at least in that part of Africa with which I am familiar, like to dress up in the same style, like a uniform. It is called 'Ashobe'. They buy bolts of cotton of a similar design or have one printed. The design may have the purpose of the occasion shown or someone's image printed on it, or indeed the patron saint of the parish. Sometimes the neckline of a dress may slice off the eye or half of the forehead of the President, or any other dignitary being honoured. Someone's face may be on an ample buttock and I once saw St. Jude standing in the cleavage of a well-endowed bosom.

Long ago, at the beginning of the last century, the French and English priests spoke the local language wherever they worked. In the 1940s – 50s secondary schools flourished in Sierra Leone. Priests moved into teaching and for the most part lost the language. The use of an interpreter became common practice. The interpreter was a formidable one-man institution. He was literate, well versed in Christian doctrine, and since he interpreted, or interrupted, all the readings and the sermon, heaven knows what version of the Word reached the people.

My favourite memory has to be about a dear friend called Mike. It was colonial times or shortly after. It was possible to order items by mail catalogue, from firms in the UK. These parcels came through the local post office, and even after paying customs duty it worked out cheaper than buying in the local shops. Wages and cost of living were closely enough related to make all this possible. Long, long ago.

Mike was the chief interpreter at the time in Serabu. He took great liberties with the sermon, embellishing wherever he thought necessary, thereby lengthening the sermon to no great advantage. If the priest began a sentence with "the Pharisees said", Mike would start: "the Pharisees . . . now these were people who thought a lot of themselves and very little of anyone else. They were also extremists for the letter of the law and had no compassion . . .well anyhow they said . . ." Then he would swing towards the priest to indicate that the next sentence was due. He wore a belt on his trousers and had a habit, when he reached the altar and turned towards the people, of straightening his tie, hitching up his trousers to somewhere around his rib cage, from where they would slip and settle in some natural conclivity in his torso, only to be yanked up again.

But this day the bishop had come and Mike went up to interpret, dressed in his best. When he turned towards us he was modelling a new tie from the catalogue and there was Marilyn Monroe stretched the whole length of it. She is alleged once to have quipped, that she had her photograph taken with nothing on but the radio. Well, there she was. But this little number had an added feature. She had two glass eyes which moved, and when Mike turned to hear better what the bishop had said, there was Marilyn making eyes at his Lordship.

Unfortunately I was not privy to the bishop's comments because Archbishop Brosnahan had a great sense of humour and was a great man for an adroit summing up. Someone asked Mike if the tie was appropriate. He was astonished. It was, he said, a very fine tie, and he had paid good money for it. So what now?

Happily for everybody the interpreter is losing his laurels; there are now local priests who are able to address their own people in their own language. The Catholic Church has come a long way from the days of the Latin Mass.

Visitors: As Serabu, like the Colony, was an isolated place visitors were always welcome. There is something about visitors – rules and routines are suspended for a while and news from the outside is like opening a window on to a new scene. Memories of visitors in childhood would come back. I shall always see Uncle Martin O'Donnell ride into the yard at mid-term break with his gun strapped to the side of his bicycle and butterscotch in his pocket for us. He never gave it all at the same time so throughout his visit there were great expectations.

Visitors to Serabu were national or international, working with different organisations and of different faiths. They enlightened, encouraged or entertained us and sometimes we pressed them into service

Dr. Carol McCormack, a medical anthropologist, came from the London School of Hygiene and Tropical Medicine. She was particularly encouraging in our growing interest in the women's initiation society (Bundo) as a possible means of furthering the health of women and children. She had done the original research on 'Madam Yoko' who was a very famous Bundo leader in Moyamba in the early part of the twentieth century. A luxury beach hotel in Freetown had been named 'The Mammy Yoko'. Carol's stamp of approval gave us the courage we needed, because not everybody approved of our association with a secret society, that in earlier years we, as Missionaries, had condemned.

Ambassadors came calling. We had asked Misereor, a German Catholic organisation to provide finance for a children's ward. They had agreed, as they used to say, in principle, but awaited a report from the German Ambassador in Sierra Leone to visit us and send them a report. I met the gentleman in Freetown and reminded him that he was to visit us. He said he would come of course. He would like very much if I could find a Bundo Mask for him. I not only got him one but got an old one from a well-known family in whose use it had been. Still there was no visit from the Ambassador. So I took up my pen and wrote, what my mother used to ask me to write on occasion, 'a nice letter' but did not fail to point out nicely that we had a bargain and I had fulfilled my part; unfortunately His Excellency had not yet done his part. A 'nice letter' came back saying that he would come next month, giving the date and time. I told the town chief that these people would be coming and he said they knew how to receive them. Then a second letter from the Ambassador – a very nice letter this time – saying that he and his wife would like to stay for the weekend and that he would be taking along the American Ambassador and his wife. Bedad! This was a nice kettle of fish.

The town had no suitable accommodation and on our compound there was one only bungalow that had two little bedrooms with a single bed each. It was the house of an elderly English lady and her two dogs. Of course we would accept them – didn't we need an X-ray as well as the children's ward? They would stew in that small house but then let them have an experience. They were to arrive in the late afternoon so an evening meal was in the plan. The chief, now quite excited about the prospect of two Ambassadors, laid everything on to receive them at the bridge below the town. We were about to have a sandwich lunch when a courier came from the town, wild of eye and short of breath, shouting: "They are here! they are here! And it's only twelve o'clock !" Clearly I was to blame and I was about to shout my defence when I perceived the parent of all Mercedes Benz, creeping towards me and behind it crawled a long low Cadillac. The town's people followed and bade them welcome and apologised for not being on the bridge. The German Ambassador said: "We were to come in the evening but sometimes the unexpected turns out best". While they were talking we had a minute to open a tin of ham and fry some chips. It would not be an ambassadorial banquet but it would do. Then someone had the misfortune to leave the dish of ham to one side whilst laying the table. When we looked around the dreadful little sugar ants of Africa were all over it. We blew them off and no one was the wiser or the worse for it. Next day we took the ladies to the local Bundo bush where they had the highest entertainment. The women danced up a dust storm and our guests sat there under the blistering sun dabbing themselves with Eau de Cologne.

For people used to higher social circles they were very gracious and appreciated everything. They also contributed generously to our entertainment with anecdotes from their own experiences in the diplomatic world. The town's people danced their legs off. We got the X-ray and the Children's Ward.

I remember another visit. I had met George and Kathy Gerardi in the US in 1970. They lived in Long Island and I would have classified them (if I had any business doing such a thing) as pretty conventional people, not given to doing adventurous things. I was wrong. They packed up and took flight for Serabu with all four children under twelve. It was, or would have been, a delightful visit if a dog had not bitten one of the children the evening before they left us. Did the dog carry rabies? There was no vaccine available. The dog looked healthy enough, the bite was a mere scratch, and on the leg, so we chose one of the ways to decide what to do: keep the dog under observation and if it is healthy at the end of ten days there is no need to worry. The family had gone to Nairobi and we were to cable them there if the dog showed any sign of illness. When, at the end of ten days, we cabled: "all is well" both the Gerardi's and we, were relieved. They more than us, naturally, not only for the child's sake but because the children's grand parents had warned, as the saying goes: "half in joke and whole in earnest", if anything should happen to the children their parents were not to come back – ever!

The only one of my family to visit was my sister Nora. She adapted to the scene with ease as we visited villages, crossed ferries, and attended local festivities. Her one fear was snakes. When I assured her that snakes do not go upstairs, she was unconvinced and searched the room every night before going to bed. It was a memorable three weeks.

10

Health Economics

How do you learn to run a hospital when you never ran anything but the chicken farm in Killeshandra and even then only fed and watered the fowl? I did know that when I put my hand under the hen, removed her egg, weighed it, and marked up the weight and the hen's number that it generated money somewhere, but I never saw the accounts. While in U.C.D. our fees were paid directly to the College. We did not even know how much our fees were. During training, we thought the doctors were well off but never heard anything about costs. Exchanges of money for services happened somewhere in space, but not in our space.

A small, fat baby boy of six months who had pneumonia was the occasion of my introduction to health economics. This was my first pneumonia in Africa. I gave him the treatment and, as with all firsts, I watched anxiously for his recovery. He got better. I was delighted.

But Sr. Breed O'Keeffe from Cork who was training me in asked: "How much did they pay for the Penicillin?" I had never thought of it.

"And now", she said, with gentle but unrelenting logic: "I'm wondering where you think the next supply of penicillin will come from."

The sum in question was seventeen shillings and sixpence. When I next saw the child's father I explained that he ought to make his own contribution to the cost of the drugs. As expected, he asked for a reduction and I gave in, thinking, "I am going to hate this life if it means I have to ask the people for money".

Dr. Margai, once more came to my rescue. He explained that the Mende are a very pragmatic people. They have a proverb which says: "If you see a man running through his own rice field, he is either being chased or is giving chase". If you do not accept something in money or in kind from, in my case the patient, he will assume you are getting some secret, concealed benefit out of it for yourself and be suspicious. Always ask for something for any services rendered as a contractual relationship between you. This establishes some equity. To act otherwise is paternalistic and unacceptable. This thinking runs right through Mende tradition.

Still, it always remained both a heartache and a headache. I used to cross the Sewa River at Sumbuya every Friday to hold clinic at a health centre there. This is a large river. During the dry season rocks and sand banks are exposed and occasionally a crocodile basks on the rocks. In the rains the river can rise thirty feet and sometimes floods the houses on the bank, though not often and not disastrously as the Sewa has a great sweep to the ocean.

We brought drugs and some minor equipment from the hospital and crossed the river in a canoe, with an outboard engine, owned by Tommy Crossover. The town itself was cut off from two hospitals by the river, consequently the clinic was always packed, one hundred patients being seen in a day. I was coherent for the first seventy people. After that I began to ask the same question twice. And we had to work very fast to make it across the river before dark. One took no chances with the Sewa. This meant that really listening to people was almost impossible, which is why Mabinty remains in my mind. I had put her on a couch in a little cubicle explaining with almost indecent haste that she needed surgery for a very large uterine tumour. As I swung away from the couch she took my hand and drew me back:

"You told me that six years ago."

"What happened?"

Apparently she had come to the hospital six years previously and having examined her I had explained that the cost of the surgery would be eight pounds. There was no bed available and there was a waiting list. She took lodging in the town where the cost of maintaining herself ate up her eight pounds.

"From that day to this" she said "I have never been able to put that much money together again." In the meantime both the tumour and the cost had increased.

In order to make up these shortfalls, which were often as high as 40%, we, like all church related hospitals and clinics, worked like beavers to make sure that 'treatment only for those who could pay' did not become a reality within our walls. To do this we were obliged to look for help inside the country and outside it in terms of both finance and senior staff. As the economy worsened the people became increasingly unable to meet the costs. We kept our heads down and worked as hard as we could to keep the costs as low as possible, not using an expensive treatment if a cheaper one would do as well. Above all, we began to look seriously at prevention, which is not only better than cure but a whole lot cheaper.

New York: Given the precarious finances in Serabu, it was inevitable that I would go to the United States. When I first arrived in New York from Sierra Leone I sat on the bed in my room and rubbed down both my arms, where for some reason I thought my misery was located. "Why", I asked the room, "Why did I leave Louisburgh in the first place, cross the ferries to Bo and Serabu and so find myself here to raise funds – to clear a building debt – here, alone, in of all places, New York?"

The reason for my misery was not hard to find. I had made no contacts, had set up no programme and only knew one or two people and was now at large in the Big Apple.

Anyway, I got myself out of debt through many experiences on TV and radio shows thanks to personal contacts and friends. Dr. and Mrs. Davidson Nicol, then Sierra Leone's Ambassador to the United Nations, had me stay with them for six weeks, believing that I would fare better if I had a base from their home. Davidson was immensely helpful and I remember him and his wife with gratitude. Matthew Ganda, from my own village of Serabu, showed me how to negotiate N.Y. Matthew was on the Sierra Leone UN Team at the time. Mrs Susan Bagley Bloom gave me the use of her office and secretary in New York. This was a big help.

I had met Susan in Freetown through the kind effort of one Mrs Victoria Jones Dove, a sophisticated elderly lady of an old Creole family, who had once been admitted at Serabu. On returning to Freetown, Mama Victoria learned that a wealthy American lady named Mrs Bloom was putting up a school of nursing in Freetown for the Ministry of Health. Mama was convinced of two things: that Serabu needed and deserved financial help and that by hook or crook she would see that I met this lady. She contacted Susan in Freetown but establishing contact with me up country was more difficult. She sent message after message via the priests in Bo that I should proceed to Freetown to meet this Mrs Bloom. I kept receiving messages from uncomprehending priests in Bo like: "for goodness sake will you go see this blooming woman!" So I did but with some embarrassment. Not being used to American heiresses and one that works with Government, I felt that she had been talked into this meeting and would not really in the least want to see a Catholic sister. We met for lunch in the Paramount Hotel in Freetown and I was pleasantly surprised to meet a perfectly amiable young woman, younger than myself, who professed interest in all health programmes regardless of who ran them. She was heading up a Foundation at the time aptly named AHEAD (American Health Education for African Development) It was late nineteen sixties and there started a friendship that has lasted the years

After I had returned to Serabu, and her project with the Ministry was concluded, Susan had another project in mind which, for a variety of reasons, did not work out. It was decided to re-deploy the funds elsewhere. Unknown to us, Susan had chosen to donate the remaining money to Serabu. Imagine my shock one day to receive a letter telling me that the sum of $103,000 had been donated. I feigned collapse. Grace and Denise quickly set up a charade of smelling salts and fans. One hundred and three thousand dollars is a lot of money at any time. This was a fortune in 1970. For Serabu that often had as little as $1500 in the Bank it was a king's ransom. We wondered how one handled that kind of money. I was despatched to Archbishop Brosnahan in Freetown for advice. He was pleased at our good fortune and told me that he had met the lady when she was in Freetown. He advised that I should see the manager of Barclay's Bank.

"What can I do for you Sister?" asked a polite junior official.

" I want to see the manager"

" Well . . . can I help?"

" I want to see the manager" I insisted. He went to a larger desk that accommodated a larger man. They whispered reverentially in the church-like way they do in these money hallowed halls.

Gently quizzical, this senior official asked what he could do for me. He was used to little missionaries who had queries that meant little enough to Barclays in terms of investments. I studied him for a minute to see if he was important enough for me. I felt like shouting:

"Today I be woman of substance. I fit see manager." but I restrained myself and instead said tentatively: " We have received a donation of some dollars and I want to know how best to invest it"

"Indeed", with a vaguely paternal smile "and how much money are we talking about?"

I told him. Oh! would I please step this way. In the end I do not know who I met but even the janitor in Barclays could have told me that it could be invested in Barclays International in London.

Which it was and used to pay for those patients who could not pay in full, or not at all, for many years.

On her frequent visits to Freetown Susan visited Serabu – "my favourite convent," she used to say and add wryly, "as if I knew another." One memory I will always cherish is the day she was helping us at a survey in Yengema village, where we were examining all children for weight and height. The old chief decided she should measure his height. Susan was working outside and I was examining children in a room of the house. I looked out and beheld Susan measuring the Chief for height. He was standing bolt upright against a palm tree, looking his absolute best, shoulders back, head up, and Susan reaching up to chart all the inches of a man who must have been very handsome in his youth. I never met a Chief who did not take the measure of a fine-looking woman, regardless of his age. I regretted not having a camera with me.

In the intervening years Susan has helped Serabu many times when funds were low enough to be at crisis point.

A White Cock: One day, as on dozens of others, I was on my way out to work when a man who had been sitting outside got up, came towards me and supporting his right arm with his left, presented his right hand roughly bandaged. His face wore the pain of the world. On undoing the bandage I found that an abscess had blown up the space between his thumb and forefinger. Pain made him cower away, untouchable. It was pointing, ready to pop, so I advised him to soak it well in warm water, gave him antibiotics and analgesics and bandaged it up. It burst spontaneously; a few more dressings and it healed or so I heard from some one in his village later.

I went to Ireland on leave, came back and it was all of eighteen months later that I was called to the back door. There was a man standing there in a lilac safari suit and white fez, holding a white fowl. Every doctor knows that patients like to be recognised and their particular problem remembered. Heavens! I said to myself who on earth is this man? Seeing my problem my present visitor just held up his right hand, separated his thumb and forefinger and there was the scar. He had perfect function. He then presented the white cock, which is traditionally an expression of great esteem. He explained that he had come to the convent rather than the hospital in the first place driven by pain and would not forget how I stopped in my tracks and attended to him; he added for good measure that he would not forget me ever.

I was really moved that one morning, so long after the event, this man had risen from his chair, called his children to chase the cock, dressed in his good clothes, and came to make this gesture. It created a great sense of wonder and warmth. We had little in common; he knew little of me or I of him, yet there he was, his gratitude like one of these myriads of small lights in windows that defy the night and light up the dark places not only in our world but in our souls.

Nor can I forget a village farming woman who came to see me in outpatients. Having paid for her medicine she returned to the consulting room, removed her headscarf, untied the knot at the end of it, extracted two coins and gave them to me, "for yourself" she whispered "for cigarettes". I received the gift graciously and managed to stop the assisting nurse from explaining that I did not smoke. "Every one, no matter how poor, has the right to be a queen from time to time", I told her.

Naval Dockyard and Farrell Lines: While in the US I went to stay with the Dominican Sisters in Rockville Centre, Long Island. One of the sisters, Katherine Gee, mentioned one evening that her brother Bill was a naval surgeon and asked whether I would accept an invitation to dinner at his home. Present also at that dinner was Ed Salsbury, also a naval doctor. They asked if I would be interested in some operating room equipment. I thought how marvellous it would be to have a larger number of instruments and supplies, so that we would not have to wait between operations for everything to be boiled up again. These gentlemen told me that, in 1945, two ships had been out-fitted with a fully equipped operating room each. The war ended before they were called into service. They suggested that I have a look at the equipment in the naval dockyard; it seems that it was now more economical to buy new equipment than to pay labour to unpack the instruments and redistribute them.

Here, for the taking, were all the instruments for general surgery, still wrapped in vaseline paper, in their pristine condition, if I could pack them. Hopping with excitement I went to the parish priest who gave me two young boys from Rockville Centre funded by Catholic Charities. I worked all that summer, unpacking and re-packing instruments, linen, gloves, catheters, syringes, stainless steel trays and dishes. I got a sense of how Imelda Marcos must have felt on her first visit to Fifth Avenue or wherever the shoes and jewellery are kept. Also in a safe was a large quantity of morphine tablets. Does anyone remember those days now? One tab was placed on a spoon with a little sterile water, the whole heated over a flame, drawn up in a syringe and injected subcutaneously. As narcotics medication was difficult to come by, this was a great bonus.

But I remembered that I should have official permission from the Chief Medical Officer to bring narcotics into Sierra Leone. So I wrote explaining the situation and kindly requesting permission to bring them with me. The gentleman in question very kindly refused. The entire consignment being already in one of 300 cartons, I was obliged to bring them anyway. What was I to do? Declare them or not?

To solve the narcotics problem, I presented myself at the Sierra Leone consulate in N.Y. and was fortunate to meet the Foreign Minister to whom I told my story. He advised me, given the circumstances, to go ahead. If by any chance the customs opened that one carton out of all the others, he would do the explaining.

There still remained the problem of financing the freight to Freetown. I was advised to go to the General Manager of Farrell Lines in New York City and ask for a container to take my precious cargo to Freetown. I got an appointment and proceeded to the rarefied atmosphere of the top suite. How I dared, I don't know. The man seemed intrigued with this strange intruder, sitting there in front of him, having the audacity to ask for a container to be put on one of his ships and deposited in Freetown – free of charge. In his chairman-like way he said: "That would be illegal, sister". Serves me right, I thought, for venturing so far out of my depth. I could think of nothing to say, but then just said: "Does that really matter?" Rallying to the human side, he sat up like a man who needed to hear the crunch of breaking rules: "You are darned right!" he said, "It doesn't". I got the container. It was deposited in Freetown and a CARE truck took it to Serabu. From Brooklyn to Serabu without costing a penny. The customs man in Freetown looked at all the cartons and called his supervisor who decreed that he should accompany the container to Serabu, which he did. After dinner and a stiff whiskey he mellowed, waved at the cartons and asked for the fastest way home.

Some months later I was travelling out of the country and at Las Palmas a bus took us across the tarmac to the plane. Who should be in the bus but the same Foreign Minister who had helped me in New York. He greeted me across the bus and added: "Did those narcotics arrive safely sister?" I thanked him, to the swivelling heads and strange stares of a number of passengers.

Bill Gee is alive and well, still working, inventing OPG machines; he loves his work so much that he scorns either a holiday or retirement. Sr. Katherine Gee OP has retired from her teaching post in Rockville Centre. Ed Salisbury retired from the Navy and when last heard of was well. The foreign minister in question still serves his country in the diplomatic service. Their combined effort served Serabu hospital well.

Gooding & Gooding Solicitors: On a few days break in Freetown I was surprised to receive a letter inviting me to attend the offices of the solicitors, Gooding and Gooding. As I searched about in my mind as to what this could possibly mean I became anxious. To me the law has always meant trouble. Have I, or the hospital, 'palaver' (quarrel) with any one I wondered? It turned out that this my first and only visit to a solicitor's office was very pleasant indeed.

The Goodings are a well-known Creole family. They received me graciously and to my surprise informed me that Serabu hospital had been left a legacy of five thousand Leones, about £2,500 at that time, by a Sierra Leonean gentleman who had died the previous year in Las Palmas. The deceased had named Dr. Eldred Jones, Principal of Fourah Bay College, and one Madam Johnson as executors. The codicil of the will did not state what, if any, connection he had with Serabu or whether he had ever been a patient there. He was obviously well informed about Serabu's activities as he left the money for the training of nurses. I tried hard to find out who he was: we looked up records at Serabu, asked priests who were a long time in the country if they knew anything of him, and visited Fourah Bay College. Dr. Jones was able to tell me that he was a quiet, unobtrusive man, a teacher and a scholar. They did not often meet but exchanged articles and documents of literary interest from time to time. Priests who were a long time in the country were no more helpful. Just one priest thought he may have been helped out with employment way back but nothing definite.

So this quiet man left what money he had to his relatives and then to three charities: Serabu Nurse Training, Masanga Leprosy Hospital and Bishop Elwin Memorial Church. I never did find out who he was. The money was used as he indicated.

We would, in normal circumstances, send reports to donors thanking them and providing an account of how the money was used. In this case we can only record the incident for its strengthening of our faith in humankind.

11

Broadening Horizons

By 1970 all the buildings I had dreamed of were in place, patients were coming from all over Sierra Leone as well as neighbouring countries.

Exhilarating days and nights of saving the life of shocked, pulse-less, ruptured tubal pregnancies had become commonplace. We could be in theatre in forty minutes from the moment the decision to operate was made. This was no mean achievement as the nurses were scattered throughout the village, and there were no telephones. Instead, the church bell was rung in a fast, urgent way and they came on the double. We had, as has been said, devised a quick and competent way of auto-transfusing these patients who had internal haemorrhage. The operation itself only takes minutes. These patients did extremely well. The "Kaye y Ngewoma" (thanks be to God) of twenty-four hours later was always a surprise. They never paid a penny, or hardly ever, because no time was lost asking for a fee before they went to theatre and afterwards . . . well . . . "Tell God tenkee!", tell God thanks. That is one way to ensure credits in Heaven and debits in the books.

Sometimes, bizarre pathology was sensational, like the five abdominal pregnancies I operated on in a three-year period. Why so many in a short time? Who knows? One was delivered alive, but I was unable to keep in touch so do not know how long it lived. Tracing people who have no postal addresses and who also move around a lot is impossible. One was living at birth but died in a few hours. A description of the others makes amazing reading, but perhaps not for here.

Then there was the quiet satisfaction of stomach by-passes for elderly male patients with pyloric obstruction. Why not female? Who knows? There was, as well, the boredom of long lists of hernias. God knows how many I have done in a life-time. Those hernias were always for old men who needed to be all ship shape before meeting the ancestors, somewhat like the king in Celtic Ireland who had to be sound in wind and limb in death as well as in life. There were also so many benign utero-ovarian tumours that it was rare to have an operating list without one. Nurse training had been established. The hospital was running well.

Information began to drift in to us from the Under Fives Clinics that we had started in 1965, as recommended by Professor David Morley, of the London School of Hygiene and Tropical Medicine. Each of five villages had a visit a week. All children under five years were weighed, immunised, and treated for intercurrent diseases. Pregnant women were examined for their nutritional state and obstetrical condition, and health education was given to all. That meant that they were advised as to what they should do, but entirely from our point of view.

Denise Dorr or Biddy O'Donohue brought sad stories week after week, from the villages they visited. There would be a story about a perfectly healthy child of eight months who had died of malaria in the absence of the team – why could the mother not have a few tablets of antimalarials in the house we wondered; another story told of a mother of five who was told she should deliver in hospital but chose not to, and died in childbirth – why? we asked, uncomprehending; another child appeared at clinic with the horrible symptoms of Kwashiorkor – were they really that poor?; another child died of dehydration following an attack of diarrhoea. So the sad and confusing stories kept coming. It seemed to be always mothers and children whose needs we were not reaching.

It was too easy to believe that, if the hospital were full, all the people who most needed care were coming. Now we discovered that this was not the case. But why did they not come? There was the distance of course, even if only three miles, but it had to be walked; there was the issue of financial resources, the management of which we did not understand at all; there was the problem of decision-making; it did not occur to us to find out who decided where a woman should have her baby. In addition, their perception of disease causality demanded at least a trial of the tried and known remedies, before they went to the hospital, which put the hospital at a disadvantage, because they often came too late.

Of course we had made a number of observations.The people had an incalculable number of herbal remedies which we dubbed 'native medicine'. I had little time for it. It was thought dangerous. Some of it is, if given inappropriately and in the wrong doses. But what humbles me now is the scant respect I had for a people who for a thousand years, had explored the medicinal properties of the green world around them and had survived – without me.

They had a great number of beliefs that militated against health, as I saw it. And so some of them do. I had no penetrative understanding of this belief system as the basis for their world and life view. I would refer to them as 'these people', meaning quite different from us. I would bewail the fact that they were stuck in their old traditions, taboos, paradigms of behaviour and wonder why they were so difficult to change?

They wore festoons of charms around their waists in pregnancy to protect them from a host of hostile forces. I can still see the rueful expression on the face of the Mende nurse as we cut them off. Hygiene? Well, true enough. Later we learned to explain to them why we were doing it and asked them where they would like them placed. We were removing their felt security, their only grip on what was sure and sacred in the bewildering strangeness of a delivery room.

And we gave them advice. We did. We told them what they ought to do about everything. Straight down the line from us to them. We planted prodigiously, but we did not explore whether our 'crops' were native to the soil, or even, if in some cases the seed might be allowed to die. "Unless the grain of wheat . . ."

To our later dismay, one crop that flourished was the people's utilisation and later abuse of medication. They seemed to have a hunger for 'medicines', both herbal and conventional and in particular they loved injections, locally called 'chuck'. They would take a chuck from almost anyone who offered it and the more it hurt the better.

The decade after the war saw the development of a great range of miracle drugs. They were halcyon days for the profession. We believed that we could cure everything. There was something new today, and there would be more tomorrow.

We were gradually creating a dependency on medicines, and on ourselves. Neither the medicines nor the doctors were the answer to malnutrition nor to water borne diseases. The indiscriminate use of western medicines was a new health hazard.

It became clear that the people whom we served and with whom we interacted daily, lived in another world than ours where skills, rituals, taboos, traditions, problem solving, values, gender issues, interpersonal relations, protocols of behaviour from birth to death, determined the way of life of each person and the community. I, and my companions, had been expecting western medical concepts to effect radical health change within a cultural reality that we did not understand. New wine into old wine-skins. It gradually became clear that we would have to go into that world and seek more enlightenment and give less advice.

A tragic incident at the hospital at the time helped. A young girl had been admitted whose labour had been so mismanaged that she had a broken back. She also had septicaemia. "Don't let me die", she begged "I am only sixteen years old". But she died. Sometimes I was sad and I have seen Lucy weep over senseless deaths like that one. In this case I was furious, and fumed: "What do those granny midwives think they are doing?", and felt like calling the police. Instead, I cooled down, assembled a delegation from the hospital and asked for an appointment with the Paramount Chief and Elders. We presented our case. They drew their gowns up on their shoulders and explained that in their culture men did not interfere in women's affairs. Then a young man, an agriculture officer in the chiefdom, spoke up:

"It is a mighty strange thing for me to hear that the chiefs are not responsible for the welfare of their people, men, women and children. We, the men here present, claim responsibility for our women."

The chief, a little shocked, then asked if we would leave the matter with them. We went home.

A week later, twelve old granny midwives from the particular area where the tragedy occurred, presented themselves at the hospital for training. I was to come to love those old women so dearly that it eludes explanation. This was a real breakthrough and gave us the courage to seek help for health where it lay – with the people themselves. We had our part to play but not alone.

We knew that working with the people would demand huge attitudinal change in ourselves and in the communities we served, but there was no other honest way.

I was tired and I took a break. A kindly providence directed me to Antwerp in Belgium for a Masters degree in Public Health.

Community Health: At that time, 1973, Antwerp/Amsterdam had a vast resource of Third World Health expertise from Zaire and Indonesia and I was, for the first time, exposed to medical anthropology, sociology, demography and statistics, as well as health economics, management, and planning. My small medical world was blown apart. The course was conducted in English and the group included Sudanese, Indonesians, West Africans, Vietnamese and Filipinos. Sharing experiences with a group like that was an education in itself.

That year was the most liberating year of my professional life and I have never looked back. Having completed the course in Public Health, I felt myself better skilled to approach the local communities in our area. Involving the people in their own health was a great about turn in health care. After all those days and nights writing and begging, and planning the building of a hospital I now come back from my studies and tell my long suffering sisters that we have not yet achieved our goal and were not even on the right road.

First we did a survey. Not scrupulously scientific, as that would need more money than we had. It was easy to say: "Go to the community" but that needed staff and a vehicle and the hospital resources were already strained. We believed that it is possible to glean useful information by asking some simple questions of a number of people and putting the information together. It was July, the height of the rainy season. People could remember a year back easily. So we asked amongst other things:
- Were you sick since last rainy season?
- if yes, what was wrong?
- what was your first line of action?

A surprising number of adults claimed that they had not been sick in a year. Maybe malaria did not count, much as a common cold would not with us. But the surprising statistic was that, of those that fell sick, 64% of them reached for what was near to hand: herbal medicine or the services of a travelling dispenser who happened to be in the village.

It is strange that we were surprised. The people live in villages of 200 – 2000 people separated from each other by two to five miles depending on the area. Only a relatively small number of the villages of our chiefdom would be within a three-mile radius of the hospital. Clearly, if a person has a temperature of 102 degrees or upwards, with pains in the back, muscles and joints, the first move will not be to undertake a two or three mile walk. The same would apply to a woman in labour. Children would have to be carried. Delay due to inaccessibility is one of the reasons why malaria kills a million children a year in the developing world.

What were we to do? We had ceased offering advice. We got together at the hospital. We discussed. We argued. The argument concerned involving the people so that the hospital personnel would not still look like the controllers of their health, but more the harbingers of information, that would enable them to take the lead in the matter themselves. 'Tapping their potential' was a phrase that kept recurring. But how were we, who had made ourselves so important, so indispensable, such performers, to do an about turn and save some face?

The best way out of a difficulty is through it. We asked the people to meet with us for some discussions, at a time convenient to them. With the grace that characterises them they agreed but, as they were farmers, the only suitable time was at night. This suited us also as we were at work all day. With Paul Harding from the Under Fives team I started visiting the villages at night. There was little point in mentioning a time. A farmer leaves the farm when it grows dark and the job in hand is finished for the day. When he arrives home he needs a wash, and a good meal washed down with fresh palm wine – the local pint. Then he is ready to talk and/or listen. Looking back it was time stolen from rest for all of us, so neither of us was at our best; sometimes when we saw old heads beginning to nod we wrapped up and went home.

We would ask questions like: "Which would you prefer when you come in from the farm: a plate of capsules – the capsule had become popular – or a plate of rice?" They were not letting us off with that. Rice of course, but there is a place for capsules too. We went through their theories of causality of disease and ours; we went through their perception of disease problems in their community, and ours. Women in these meetings were slow to speak but would point out children's problems like neonatal tetanus, measles and whooping cough all of which were, at that time, a terrible scourge. But neither the women nor the men would mention maternal mortality rates. A mixed meeting would not be the place. The men would criticise our over involvement with women and children to the exclusion of their problems, particularly those that were sex related. They would punch each other, their mouths full of laughter in the way that men laugh about such things. And sanitation. Water can be a bearer of bacteria causing gastro-intestinal problems. Oh yeh? What about us? We are old men drinking this water all our lives and we are alive and well. What about children who die of gastro enteritis? Humph! Everybody knew, they told us, that if the mother is unfaithful to her husband while breast-feeding the child will suffer from diarrhoea. The fact that one of them sitting there might be the other partner in an illicit affair would not surface. Instead some elder, hitching up his gown on his shoulder, would pontificate: "That kind of loose living is not acceptable in our community". Derisive smirks on the women's side. To keep this fable going suited the men, because the aggrieved husband could take the case to court and a fine imposed on the offending party increased his income. The infuriating thing about that particular custom is that significant amounts of money changed hands, much more than would have provided safe drinking water in the first place, or reversed the dehydration which is the usual cause of death in diarrhoeal disease.

These sessions could not go on forever but we did visit every sizeable village in the chiefdom over a year. I have a great nostalgia for those evenings in the villages. Sometimes they were uproarious and sometimes poignant, as when an old man explained that their grand fathers had identified their particular village water source and it would be unlucky to depart from the ancestor's choices. A teacher had told him that it was unsafe for drinking. I explained gently that the water was good, it was in fact a spring coming out of a rock, but that the village garbage nearby was the problem. The first rains would wash the rotted garbage into the water and make it unsafe for drinking. Sometimes information-sharing was effective, but not always.

Gradually we became aware of the nature of the sociological soil where we wished to plant health. We learned that social health, seen as the root cause of most illness, was taken care of by an exquisite complex of rites, rituals, taboos and protocols. We discovered that the traditional administrative structure of Paramount Chief, Speaker, Section Chief, and Town Chief is the formal way into community, but that the real influence, in areas of interest to us, may lie elsewhere. It may, for example, be with one of the many secret societies. The Paramount Chief relates to these with great delicacy; none can function without his approval, but his jurisdiction is carefully orchestrated by oral tradition.

We came to know the women of the Bundo Society or, as it is called in Mende, 'Sande'. For the women, Sande is where the influence is. This is clear from the religious nature of acquiring the gift to initiate, and the sophisticated protocol for interviewing the 'Sowui', or leader of the Sande. We learned about families, polygamous and other, and the interdependence of the extended family, and also of the intricacies of decision-making that have an effect on health.

We knew then that change would take a long time and a lot of patience. Change? What needed to change? What could be changed? How were we to discern? Personally I wanted to work within the reality I met, improve on it where possible and let things come in their own time. Working with community is very different from clinical work. Although the work could take place in idyllic settings, the hospitality princely, and the 'craic' as good as in any pub in Ireland, meetings could run very late. Fatigue takes its toll. Acceptance of proposals was sometimes feigned for friendship sake, and this often took a long time to sort out. Travelling itself carries its own risks, with mosquitoes, black fly and dangers on land and sea. Hardest of all, however, is the bleak absence of fast, visible and palpable results.

Health Committees: I do not remember quite how village health committees came to be. The idea was born of the need to have some sort of functioning cell within the community that would relate to, and be supervised by, mobile teams of community health nurses. There was a slogan abroad at the time: "Health for the People, by the People" and the barefoot doctors of China were greatly talked about. We were to learn not to import schemes that worked in another country as every country is different. We had also to learn how to use skills that were already in the village. Story-telling, drama, role plays, dance and song competitions are great means of imparting health information, which in turn puts the community in possession of knowledge for their own decision-making in health matters. Story telling is one of the great arts in a community where the tradition is an oral one.

After much discussion, and many proposals and counterproposals, the first health committees came into being. On the health committee there was a chairperson, a person responsible for town-sanitation, an agriculture man, a woman who would look out for the affairs of women and children, a secretary, and one person who would be trained to use a few basic medicines so that, when malaria struck, the appropriate treatment would be available and death be prevented. Job descriptions were developed with them and each one trained for their job. We had wondered about a secretary. The literacy rate is low. We need not have worried. People who had been to school a long time ago were only too pleased to display their writing skills.

To relay the story of these committees would take a long time. They had a hard time of it. No prophet is accepted in his own country. At a night meeting once in Yengema a teacher, with a few drinks in, looked askance at the primary school drop-out who was secretary and said: "You health people, you are just a bunch of talkers. Meetings! That's all you do."

"Well let me ask you something", said the secretary, "Are you aware that in four years this village has not had a maternal death, not one single case of tetanus of the new-born . . .?"

"How do you know that?"

"Here is the births and deaths book and here are the minutes of the meetings and here . . ." and he proudly showed the few little shabby exercise books with the dog-eared edges, the squiggly writing and incredible spelling. Defeated, the teacher withdrew. I was prouder of those books than of the Book of Kells.

For some time the committees were not given enough responsibility or perhaps authority from the Chief. Many of the chiefs were old and delegated the chairmanship, but not too old to keep a wary eye on a possible pressure or power group, other than themselves, in the village or town. Also health is unexciting. If people are healthy, there is no problem. If they fall sick and are cured, this is drama, particularly if surgery is involved. But the committees persevered and since then have gone through many changes. More women than men took their places on the committees as time went on. They prepared for the visit of the hospital team, weighed the babies, kept and managed some essential medicines, even keeping records by counting stones for the number of common problems encountered. They sent messages to the hospital if they had a maternity case needing the ambulance and were in every way more caring, than their male counterparts. Though, in fairness it should be said, that it was hard-riding or hard-running young men who brought messages for help to the hospital. Health Committees made much progress from those early days and are now in common use in many countries for primary health care.

Preventive health care is hard to sell. This is not confined to Africa. In spite of many words said and written about all kinds of independence and liberation, it seems dependencies come more easily – on drugs, health providers, money, fame or family. Nevertheless there are always signs of vitality, signs that people do rise up and take their part, par-take in managing their own lives.

12

A Second Spring

In the late 1970's and early 80's Serabu Hospital was well organised and well staffed. There was a ommunity health department staffed by Sierra Leonean public health nurses, a state enrolled community health nurse training programme, run conjointly with the Methodist Mission Hospital in Segbwema and the training of traditional birth attendants was established. I was ready to spread my wings.

In 1981, a group of German Nationals, representing a bi-lateral German organisation called Gesellschaft Technishce fur Zusammenarbeit came to see me. They were preparing an integrated rural development project for Bo and Pujehun Districts, a population of 375,000, of which one component would be health. Had I any suggestions or recommendations for the health component, they wanted to know. My dissertation for the Master's in Public Health was on the "Optimisation of the Government's extensive network of Rural Health Units". As a non-government church organisation I had no access to these units, but had long nursed a secret desire to become involved. I presented my conviction so enthusiastically that I was offered the job as manager of the health programme. This was cleared with my Congregation; Dr. Belmont Williams, Chief Medical Officer, gave her approval on behalf of the Government.

The idea, that the individual and community were an essential part of a successful health service, had gained ground in hundreds of small places like ours, long before the Alma Ata declaration to that effect in 1978. The concept that people would be invited to take responsibility for their own health and that of their community and be involved in planning services that pertained to them, became known as Primary Health Care. The essential elements of this concept were that Health Services would be for all the people, would be acceptable to them, accessible and at a cost they could afford. Few ideas, if any, have ignited hopes for real change in health status, as did this. Here, at last, people believed, was the formula that would reduce infant and maternal mortality rates, and the high morbidity figures for preventable diseases such as diarrhoea and malnutrition, that were so debilitating in the rural communities where most of the people lived. Many euphorically believed that it would be easy, cheap and effective. The concept was incontestable but how to implement it was the problem.

The situation in Sierra Leone, as in many other countries with a low economy, was that there was a numerically impressive network of health centres and health posts. They were not functioning on PHC principles. Lack of spending on the health sector had left the peripheral health units (PHUs) way behind on repairs, drug supplies, on-going education, supervision and basic equipment.

The Serabu experience had taught me that revitalising the rural health units was not a 'fix it' job. It was an undertaking to provide information that would, hopefully, induce attitudinal change, not only in health professionals, but also in health related sectors like agriculture, education, social welfare and, of course, among the people at large as well. Bringing the village people on board rocked all sorts of boats. The people themselves, when told they could do a lot about their own health, found it hard to believe the professionals, suspecting they were being abandoned. Some professionals, on the other hand, felt that PHC was a cheap solution thought up for the third world by foreign experts.

Fortunately for me, the Ministry of Health instituted a task force, of which I was a member, to study the situation and plan the way forward. I was involved in workshops that were organised across the country to introduce Primary Health Care. The task force later became the planning committee, where policies and plans were drawn up for village, district and provincial health services. Another fortunate coincidence for me was that a training programme for a new cadre of health worker, to take charge of the health centres, was already under way. This category, who were to be called Community Health Officers would be trained in primary health care principles and practice and would have, among others, management, clinical medicine, immunisation, community motivation and mobilisation skills. The Ministry of Health had procured the services of Drs Iain and Riitta Liissa Aitken through ODA, Britain, to set up the new school. Using the experience of a broad spectrum of field workers and available statistics, the country's ten priority health problems and their causes were identified. The school, called the Paramedical School, opened in 1983, with Dr. Victor Cole as principal.

The detailed story of all the activities of this period is beyond the scope of these pages. They were years of extraordinary exuberance for me. I had, for the first time in my life, a budget and trained staff. I knew nothing about civil service procedures and the importance of the 'letter to the effect'. On more than one occasion I inadvertently crashed through the red tape that holds things together from, as my driver used to say, 'time memoriam'. I salute the Ministry of Health staff for their patience with me and, with the exception of a few glorious rows, soon forgotten, I established good relationships and have very pleasant memories of that time and the people with whom I worked.

In spite of being involved in a whirl of activities: building, renovating, setting up pharmacy services, ably helped by my old friend from Serabu, Henry Moriba; attending workshops, lecturing at the Paramedical School and attending innumerable meetings, I kept my sights on the Peripheral Health Units for which I had joined the project in the beginning. I set about retraining the existing peripheral health unit staff, bringing them to Bo monthly, for the first two years. Here again I was fortunate to have the help of Dr. RoseMary McMahon who had been lecturing in the Liverpool School of Tropical Medicine and Hygiene, and was in Bo at the time. Ministry of Health personnel contributed to the training, according to their particular skills. The training was kept closely in line with that of the Community Health Officers so that the old order and the new would meet on equal footing.

As there were twenty-seven chiefdoms stretching from water logged southern Pujehun to the hills of northern Bo, supportive supervision had to be carefully scheduled. Supervision provided not only on-site training for the peripheral health unit staff but also checking on buildings and renovations, some of which were done by a local contractor, Mr. Emmanuel Tommy, and some by the community.

A health centre in Sierra Leone is, on average, about the size of a small rural health centre in Ireland. The difference between them is two-fold: functions and equipment. Health centre activities include: screening of children under five years for nutritional and immunisation status and therapy for any intercurrent diseases encountered; screening of prenatal women for general health and possible at risk factors which determine whether the child will be born at the centre or in hospital; sick people are treated on the spot or referred to hospital depending on the nature of the problem; last but by no means least, in primary health care terms, is the outreach to villages or satellite clinics within a ten mile radius. Health committee members in outreach villages assist the centre team to carry out the necessary activities; training and information sharing forms a core activity at all levels in the primary health care philosophy.

The second difference is that equipment and supplies are minimal by western standards. There is neither electric light nor running water. The furniture is locally made, tables, chairs, benches, and cupboards. Equipment consists of a few buckets for fetching and storing water, ordinary cooking pots for sterilising on a three stone fire, four or five stainless steel dishes, a blood pressure apparatus, a thermometer or two, syringes, needles, a small supply of linen, charts and records, at least two storm lanterns, kerosene and candles. UNICEF provided a refrigerator and the sterilising equipment for the immunisation programme. Drug supply was strictly limited to drugs that were relevant to the main diseases encountered.

The minimum staff at a centre was the Community Health Officer, who was, in most places, the only state qualified person; an endemic disease control assistant, a mother and child health aide responsible for midwifery, and a porter. The porter was usually illiterate but served a very useful function: he carried firewood, fetched water, cleaned the premises and, very importantly, was a local of the area. He personified the local 'Who's Who'.

To establish diagnoses the Community Health Officer used his small diagnostic skills and his wits; to establish a good team spirit he held staff meetings, at which were arranged the staff time tables, and the outreach schedules; problems arising either in the community or among the staff were addressed. The overall goal was to change the health status in the chiefdom assigned to him.

There were problems facing him and his staff. Firstly, he had to be careful not to behave in a superior fashion with village people, just because he had three years third level education; secondly, some of his staff would have preceded him in the post and had their own way of doing things which he might be hoping to change: an elderly mother and child health aide whispered dourly to me one day, "I am old enough to be his mother"; and thirdly, he would be in trouble if he failed to refer patients to hospital in time, though there were villages where a truck visited only once in two weeks. Only the young would take on such a job. About 80% of them did very well and, in the decade that I was there, there were verifiable changes in health. Due to the combined efforts of the Ministry of Health, UNICEF and the Bo/Pujehun Project the ten priority diseases originally targeted had changed dramatically. With 'all hands on deck' the immunisation programme made a significant impact on measles, poliomyelitis, tetanus, whooping cough and tuberculosis.

To say there were another ten diseases lined up to be addressed is an understatement but it was great to take down the original list, which had been posted in every health centre, and tackle a new one. This time the village communities were in on the planning. Malaria and gastrointestinal disease control were more intractable but success begets success and confidence was growing.

My best memories are of visits to the centres. One day on a supervisory visit to a centre I noticed that one section town was crossed off the outreach schedule. I inquired for the reason. There was a nurse there, the community health officer said, who had set up an unapproved centre and was doing surgery. This was strictly illegal and the officer and his staff did not want even to be seen there. They were, however, most anxious that Mama Hilary herself would go there and see the situation. I found out later why they wanted me to go there. I called on the 'surgeon' and discovered that it was true, that this male, state enrolled nurse had done a Caesarean section on a makeshift kitchen table and it was also true, to my amazement, that the mother was alive and well. The perpetrator of this and other inappropriate initiatives, was answering my questions and smiling at me in a disarming fashion. I considered his attitude incomprehensible, given that he was in big, big, trouble. Finally, I said suspiciously: "Where were you trained"? "Serabu, Sister". Now Mama Hilary was looking for cover. He was not one of those I remembered. The skilled ones would never have done such a thing. I reported the situation to the Principal Medical Officer's Southern province, Dr. George Komba-Kono who went there, shut the place down, suspended the young man for a period, and thus put paid to his surgical aspirations.

The training of the mother and child health aides was updated. The district health sisters, with Onita Samai and Audry Peters, a Canadian volunteer, did Trojan work. The mother and child health aide in turn became a trainer of traditional birth attendants. I had wonderful visits to some of the traditional birth attendants. One night in southern Pujehun where I was staying over night a very elderly traditional birth attendant came to chat. "Would you like to come and see my place?" she asked. I gladly accepted. It had been a rain sodden day; the night was cloudy lacking moon or stars. We crossed a wooden bridge over a sluggish river that looked black and menacing in the dark. Arriving at her house I found it was at another waterside. It was difficult to make out whether it was river, lake or ocean. It amazed me that villages managed to stand on such sandy soil. Some had to move during the monsoons but would come back in the dry season. They had a good fishing industry. 'Mama Nurse' as she was called locally, was leading me with a bush-lamp and we went into the house. It seemed very dark to me but Mama was finding her way and showing me her 'equipment'. She had not yet been trained and all she had, in a little bag, was a clean razor blade to cut the umbilical cord, and a piece of string to tie it. I was lavish in my praise of how neat her place was and God knows she deserved it all. Then out of the bag she drew something special. "It makes the baby come out real fast" she confided. To my horror I saw an ampoule of Syntocin, a dangerous uterine stimulant, only used under skilled supervision in hospital situations. Mama was forbidden by government regulations to have that or any other injections. Down here in the last reaches of the district, many watery miles from medical help, she could have done incalculable damage. I was obliged to take it from her. I explained how it worked and enlisted her help in discouraging other women from using it. I felt bad having to do this, feeling that I was betraying her confidence. Later, in better light, I noticed the expiry date was so long past that the drug was probably harmless anyway.

I vividly recall an evening visit to another traditional birth attendant, this time in Bo district. It was dusk, it was orange blossom time and the air was balmy, cool and fragrant. Her community had built a small house for this lady in which she had one room for herself and was therefore always easily on call. She had been provided with a small, but adequate kit for deliveries, containing a foetal stethoscope, scissors, two forceps, a little cotton wool, and disinfectant. They sometimes used the local 'poiteen' as a disinfectant to swab the umbilical cord. That particular beverage was so potent that it was better for rubbing than for drinking. She took everything out to show me, as they always did. They were all in order. She had clean water from the well and a three stone fire and wood ready. This lady was in the honours class. I felt privileged to be there. As I prepared to leave she said: "Wait! The notebook Sister!" In a little exercise book, she had recorded the deliveries of the previous month. I read with surprise: "Para five three alive. Labour last six hour. Baby Boy. Normal delivery. Small blood-loss. Mother and baby fine" Knowing her to be illiterate, I questioned her.

"Who is writing this for you Mama"? Proudly she answered: "My grandson. He is in secondary school".

"He will one day be a specialist in maternity work" I declared:

"By the grace of God", she whispered. And, for sure, they will need the grace of God, as they thread their way between the old ways and the new.

Secret Societies: At first I was bitterly opposed to the members of the Bundo Society whose ideas on the management of human illness went so contrary to mine. Their particular area of expertise was in obstetrics, and evidence of their mismanagement, which I had encountered in Serabu Hospital, appalled me.

Added to that, their initiation rites included female circumcision at or about puberty and with this I disagreed. I tried with all my might to dissuade Christian girls from going through this initiation, but to no avail.

Gradually I came to know these women personally. There was Mama Yema who needed surgery. She was very much afraid of the whole idea and, having signed for it, lived unhappily with her decision for some forty-eight hours. As the time for surgery came, fear erupted. Mama took to her heels, into the bush, clothed only in a theatre shift that covered nothing at the back, and the nurses in hot and raucous pursuit. Re-assured, she was advised to reconsider, take her time and report back when courage re-visited her. She did just that and the memory of the escapade became a bond. Visiting her village later she would hug me in gales of laughter. I discovered that she was the Sowui, or head Bundo woman for her area, that she conducted initiations and was a woman of great prestige.

We talked. She invited me to enter the Bundo Bush or secret enclosure; I invited her and her colleagues to the operating room, for a Caesarean section, my own secret bush. We began to revise Dr. Margai's old training programme. In this way a long and warm association with these wonderful women began. They have established rites of passage from adolescence to adulthood for their young women. They have bonded themselves into a powerful sorority in a male controlled and dominated society and have clawed out for themselves rights and privileges. I still do not agree with some of their practices, including female circumcision, but the close-knit hierarchy, the great sense of belonging, the possibilities of rising in the ranks, the religious significance of the whole are greater than anything I was able to offer at that time – or even now.

Having taken the trouble to acquaint myself with the method of gaining access to their enclosures I became quite familiar with many of the local ladies. In particular I enjoyed being invited to the graduation – to use an American term – of the initiates, feasts of eating, dancing and singing. Oh those dances! At first I tried to follow the steps, only to conclude that my Bundo society sisters had a ball and socket joint somewhere in the spine which I lacked. Eventually it came to me that the dance is not about steps at all. It is about rhythm; about letting the rhythm flow through you and abandoning your body to it. Then it becomes a small ecstasy. I loved those dances.

One day a young woman invited me to her village to see something wonderful. She had been gifted – graced – to receive two Bundo masks from the stream where she *herself had lain under water for twenty-four hours*. The Bundo Mask is a carving of a young woman's face, a remarkably serene face, with layers round the neck representing the puppy fat of puberty. It is worn by the Bundu Devil/Spirit on formal Society occasions. After this miraculous intervention the young woman had graduated to becoming a Sowui and was, herself, approved to conduct initiation rites. No mean happening. She led me into the Society house and gave me a small stool to sit on. Other members had gathered. We settled down. She wanted to show me the masks and to tell me her story. In fact she subsequently had it written out lest I forget it.

She drew a white headscarf and a white shirt or blouse from under the rug on her bed and put them on – her uniform she said. As with all stories it began a long time ago:

"My Grandmother was the Senior Sowui of Kakua Chiefdom, Bo District. I spent my childhood days with my grandmother in the Bundo Bush. The house was like this one", she explained.

'This one,' like all other Society houses, is situated at the end of the town or village with its only opening towards the bush. It is constructed in mud and wattle, with an earthen floor and either a thatched or zinc roof. A fence of palm leaves surrounds the enclosure. A palm leaf door sometimes guards the entrance. There is often a large tree in the middle of the enclosure. Trees hold an important place in the spirituality of the people, as they did in ancient Ireland.

"After the visit of the Queen of England in 1961, I was initiated. After that I got married and went to Freetown and lived with my husband. Twelve years later when I used to go to the market I would feel dizzy and would rush home. My husband used to ask what's wrong with me, whether I am going off my head. This dizziness lasted for a month. One Friday morning I went to the market. I was unable to buy. I was confused, uneasy and worried. I returned home. My husband told me that he is taking me back home to my parents because I am behaving like a crazy woman. On Saturday he brought me back to my parents and told them that he was tired of the way I am behaving. Let them take me to a herbalist/Alpha-man." The 'Alpha-man' is a local Muslim cleric who, in addition to his

religious function, prescribes herbal or ritual cures.

It seemed it was not uncommon for husbands to return misbehaving wives to their families. She continued:

"I was taken to Pendembu in the Eastern Province to a herbalist/Alpha-man. I stayed in Pendembu for one month. No improvement. They used to smoke me morning and evening, gave me herbs and lasmamie (holy water used in the Muslim tradition) to drink. I did not get any better. He told my mother that he has cast lots, and found out that I have devils.. My mother and myself returned home. A few days after our return, I dreamt about the masked devils talking to me, describing to me where I would find them, take them from the water and bring them to the Bundo Bush. They told me that I should pay Leones 42.00, all in coins, ten cents and one cent – and throw all into the stream and dress in white – docket (blouse), lappa (wrap around skirt), pants, and head scarf.

"On a Friday evening I started to shiver as though I had high fever and ran out of the house like a mad woman, down to the stream where the villagers get their drinking water. I was directed to that particular stream by the devils. I slept under the stream; the women who had followed me continued singing throughout the night. I got out of the water the next day at about 1 p.m. with one mask devil in my hand and the women shouted Hoyoo . . . Hoyoo! Sign of shouts of joy.

"I was told by the masked devil to build a new house and it should be a round house and this was done in a week by the community."

I made a wry mental observation, that community activities, undertaken for health or economic progress drag along interminably but for a religious purpose are completed in a week. " *And now*", she said, *"would you like to see the stream where all this happened"?* Five people, two of them Europeans, expressed our sense of privilege at the offer. She led the way along a footpath that wriggled its way through dense bush on either side, making a green coolness. Long necked palm trees reached for the sky above the bush here and there. Presently we arrived at the pool. It was not deep and measured some three metres in diameter. Young bamboo trees making Gothic arches over it provided a sense of the sacred. The beauty silenced us. This lady, now a Sowui, waded into the water to mid calf. She spoke to the spirit residing there, giving him our names and asking for specific blessings for each one of us. Now she said, *"If he answers, the water will move"*. We waited in reverent silence for this priestess of the forest to wrest blessings for us from her 'Devil/Spirit'.

The waters did not move, but as she quietly said, *"Not today,"* a bird sang out right over our heads and she cried: *"He has answered!"*

I reflected long on this experience. "Do you believe it Sister?" someone whispered. I felt a sense of God's dealing with people. Some of these were Biblical themes, and some, reminiscent of other religious traditions:

- water immersion/transformation
- the moving of the water
- a change of name
- a uniform /habit
- the song of a bird
- the assuming of a role.

Was there something here I wanted to change or that needed change? What could I offer instead? Surely this woman had experienced God's healing power in the events of her life. At the time of my meeting with her she was, and had been, working in good health for several years.

Of the initiation rites for men I knew very little. The Porro society turns boys into men they say. It is strictly taboo for women to be inquisitive about it. To actually see the Porro Devil is severely punishable but in what way I never knew. I just took good care to keep out of his way when he was about.

About the other men's society I know even less as it is very secret, and very powerful. It was the old warrior society, and is called the Wunde Society. I was once privileged to see one part of their initiation rites and was amazed to see that the initiates were dressed as women. This was not explained to me. My only brush with it was when I had a patient once who was terminally ill and in great pain, a Christian and an ex-teacher. His family arrived in a truck to take him home to die in the sacred bush. I knew his village and had experienced travelling the road there. It would rattle the teeth in your head, fling you from one side of the vehicle to the other and leave you feeling you had had a bout with Mike Tyson. So I pointed out that the patient would not live more than a few days and asked whether they would not wait and let him die in whatever comfort we could offer him. No! He must come! He must die in the Wunde Bush in his village. They stood strongly against any reason I was able to offer. The patient himself begged that I would keep him. He was in pain and knew that whatever help he could get was in the hospital. Holding on to my hand he pleaded: "Don't let me go! Don't let them take me!". I thought I could persuade them. There was a male nurse, one of our church members, from that area who was an initiate of the same secret society that now demanded the patient's last hours in their midst. I spoke of Christian compassion and of the rights of the individual, of the patient, to make his own decisions.

"How could you", I pleaded, "put a dying patient in a truck on that road?"

I was told that I should know better and that the Wunde Society is a warrior society; children do not join it. Young men make this choice and freely abdicate some of their rights and take on a commitment to the society and its rules. He has enjoyed its privileges during his life. He now must honour his obligations.

They took him away. I sedated him heavily. But it fairly broke my heart when they returned from the village telling me that, when the old man reached the village, he lifted his head, looked around, laid it back again and said: "So Sister let me go!"

Favourite Villages: Mongama lies some four miles west of Serabu. There was a pathway that loped in gentle curves through the bush, fell into streams at various places and rose again to repeat the process and eventually find Mongama. Parts of the way bore testimony to varied but failed efforts, at different times, to establish a road which would shorten the distance from Bo to Serabu and offer benefits to the villages of transport for goods and people. The road never materialised because it was impossible for the village people to make a four-mile road and do their regular farming work at the same time, without some assistance from the Department of Works. This never came. So we all walked.

The village numbered some four hundred people and boasted illustrious well known individuals who, as lawyers and teachers, served their country with honour.

This town was designated a Section town and had the usual structure of Section Chief, Speaker and Town chief. Both Porro and Bundo initiations were conducted there, smaller villages in the area amalgamating for these functions. No matter how small the village, there was always the same governing structure. We had a health committee in Mongama who got together to build a small house that would serve as a health post where meetings could be held, immunisations and treatment sessions conducted as and when necessary. It measured about thirty feet long and was divided into two rooms. A neat palm-leaf thatch made it cool and we were very glad of it when working there. I was the first to sleep in it. It was heavenly, as the mattress grass was fresh and its gentle fragrance was evocative of new mown hay in The Colony long ago. But maybe the reason I slept so well was that we stayed up late telling stories: stories of the great ancestors who were prominent in the hut tax war; of battles fought by the forefathers of Mongama to acquire this land; and, of course, tales of which families were brought in as captives and were not really Mongama people, and so on.

The purpose of our work in this village was for the people to reconsider their notions of health and to look intensively and seriously at what lay in their own power to keep themselves healthy. Up to now we had been telling them that they had to come to the hospital for everything – they were beginning to believe us – and now we are saying "it's not true, you can manage a lot at home but perhaps not the way you were doing it before". The people received this information with a certain amount of caution and immediately assured us of their full confidence in the hospital and wonderful people like myself. Is there a Blarney Stone in Sierra Leone? So began session after session with the Health Committee, providing information that would help them to discover what they could do and how limited the hospital alone was for total health.

The committee, on learning of water borne diseases, motivated the community to dig a well. I loved wells. When I was eight years old I determined that I was going to have a well for myself. So I went secretly to the paddock with my shovel and began to dig. The paddock was a soggy boggy field where it was hard to believe that any animal was ever kept there for it would give rheumatism to a duck. Ten inches of digging yielded a few inches of water. Next came the cement because it was going to be lined with cement. Nowhere in my memory is there a cement-lined well, so where on earth did I get this idea? Having befriended one of the workmen, who was engaged in some building project for my father, I succeeded in wheedling out of him a half a bucket of cement and tottered off to my secret place. I had stood around watching the manual dexterity with which the men picked up the plaster on the front of the trowel, smacked it on to the wall and smoothed it out with the back of the trowel. Having arrived at the site I tried: pick up, slap on and then thslop . . . The cement fell into the water. Not one bit of cement stuck. Given that drinking water was from the river, that there was no shortage of it and that nobody had talked of digging a well, it is astonishing that the details of this, my first well ever, have remained so clearly in my mind. All my life in Sierra Leone water supplies were from wells: wells for the hospital, wells for the convent, wells in the villages. Can coming events cast their shadows so far before them?

At Mongama the well was dug. The use of it was another thing. Not everybody was going to convert spontaneously. I met a woman collecting water from a mossy pool under the trees and I indicated my belief that the well was there to be used. She tossed her head and told me that this water was sweeter to the taste and what is more, she added: "It's cooler and I don't have a fridge". A direct hit.

Once there was a bucket crisis. The bucket, which alone was to be dipped into the well, disappeared for a while so nobody had access to the water. It turned out that the man who had given the bucket for the use of the community had not consulted his wife. The good lady berated him and took her bucket away. It took our nurses a long time to unearth the truth and then how was it to be solved? It was the time of the Camp David meeting in the U.S and as this debate dragged on and on the thought occurred to me that this bucket was causing as much trouble as the Arab-Israeli crisis. In the end it was decided that the whole village would make a contribution and give the money to the lady who then, graciously, gave back the bucket and bought a new one for herself. So the husband was vindicated and the wife got a bucket. Every one then roared with laughter, the chief called for the palm wine, and we all had a 'pint'.

Another problem arose for which the committee called on our help. They had learned that goats and sheep could be reservoirs of the dreaded tetanus spore; they should be tethered while grazing and corralled when in the village. If not they tended to wander on to the verandas and their droppings contaminated the area. The young student nurse who was to present the problem, stood in front of the chief, dripping with respect, hands behind his back, explaining about the dangers of tetanus and how good it would be if the goats in question were corralled. No one present showed a flicker of emotion. The goats in question were, of course, the chief's. The chief responded in accents so comprehending and co-operative that no one lost face, everyone felt a winner – but the goat problem only went away for a short time. It was like that in nearly every village. Some problems you learned to live with.

At Mongama the Sande women were the first to invite me inside their enclosure, the Panquima, and the first to attend a Caesarean section in the operating theatre to see for themselves just how it was and where the baby could have problems on this its first journey into the world. It was Mama Kema who told me that when a woman died in child-birth a post mortem Caesarean was done and mother and child were buried side by side in a special place in the bush, the place thus becoming sacred forever.

Hospitality among the village people in Sierra Leone is legendary. I am told it is so with all traditional farming people. Mongama at any rate was five star. The staple food is rice which is served in a bowl separate from the sauce that goes with it. The sauce is called 'plasas' and contains a protein, normally fish, green vegetable, beans and red palm oil. But, for guests, there is always chicken, cooked in a vegetable oil with pepper and various delicious herbal flavourings. Sometimes for a team, the rice would be turned onto a large, circular dish and plasas dished out on top of it. Each one is given a spoon and tucks in from their own side of the mountain. Young people do not dare go for the succulent contents of the plasas, leaving that initiative to their elders. It would be a serious breach of etiquette to do so. If it is chicken, to be offered the gizzard is a sign that the chicken was cooked specially for that particular guest. Having a great failing for gizzard, I could always do it justice. Amongst the palm oil dishes my favourite was potato leaf that always contained large flat beans. In places where my failing for potato leaf was known, it would always be the dish of the day. In situations where a large contingent of visitors was expected, such as a visit from government officials, accompanied by the usual entourage that travels with such people, the men would go hunting the day before. They would bring in deer, squirrel and other bush animals and sometimes monkey. The latter would not be offered to all guests as not all tribes eat it. Some do, some do not, and some do and say they do not. I had monkey soup once but did not like it for its very strong taste. I often wonder from where I inherited my catholic palate. Hardly in Mayo. I can eat, and enjoy, almost anything served up me.

Another village I loved was Blama. A tiny little village of no more than four or five houses, tucked away in the forest, it lies about a mile from the hospital as the crow flies. To reach there however one has to go for nearly a mile on the main road, then turn left, taking a footpath through the forest. Depending on the season, something will be in blossom. Coffee, whose berries grow in clusters along a branch, blossoms in snow-white flowers, reminiscent of melting snow on winter boughs. The blossoms are wondrously fragrant. Driving through a coffee farm in blossom time is almost overwhelming. The fragrance of orange blossoms is well known but coffee blossom was a surprise to me. From January to June the forest is full of varied fragrances. In the morning water lilies open shyly to the sun and turn an unpretentious swamp into a dream lake. But one must not, head in air, abandon oneself to an idyllic aroma-therapy session. Snakes are always a possibility and in the evening come on to pathways to digest their food, or so I am told. Another feature of the path to Blama that needs careful negotiation is a large swamp. Sierra Leone is blessed with rich inland valley swamps, good for agriculture but a problem to pedestrians. In the dry season, at its deepest, it will reach to the knees, but during the rains the middle can flow briskly and reach waist high. The way in and out of this swamp is marked by a long, black muddy area that oozes pleasantly between the toes, and leaves the legs mud-splattered to the knees. One evening as I entered there was a woman coming out. She was pregnant, and had a child on her back while a third was swimming. I used this story for the training of field workers. Walking to villages on health duties is rarely their favourite occupation. If the women walk out to clinic, staff can walk in to visit them when necessary.

This village served as a useful place to bring national or international planners. It kept them from coming up with plans that were no better than fairy stories as far as the villagers were concerned. One 'expert' is remembered as stepping gingerly into the swamp with oh! such white feet and saying: "What about Bilharzia?" To which someone answered, I thought rather brutally: "What about it?"

Sometimes on an evening off we would go to Blama for a walk, a visit or a chat. On this particular evening my companion and I, having negotiated the swamp, arrived in the village and sat chatting in the pretty little barri they had built for their health worker. They had said to her: "If your supervisors ever come they will know that you have accomplished something"

Night and day change places rapidly at that latitude, giving a very short twilight, but one of great splendour. The sun, a blood red, orange or gold orb slips away, literally while you watch, and sheds a profusion of gentler shades on the earth and sky like an evening blessing. It is the time when the day's work is drawing to a close, night and rest are approaching – the time for quiet reflection. The glossy foliage of the coffee trees around us was still, chickens pecked about happily; an old woman was spinning cotton and small children wandered, circumspectly, from their father's knees to ours, took a look at us and ran back to Papa, while others played vociferously not too far away.

We exchanged news and views. A comfortable silence enveloped us. An old man cleared his throat, looked about him and said: "I feel very happy this evening and I feel the ancestors happy too. You people must love us very much to come through that muddy swamp to be with us". The remark was so patently an awareness of the ancestors' presence and of a simple uncomplicated faith alive in his depths that it struck a live chord somewhere within me. In Mende his expression indicates a gut feeling not a thought or an insight. He felt them happy.

As I walked home in the green golden evening I was almost walking into the trees from wondering whether the Communion of Saints, which I profess to believe was as much a reality for me as the ancestors were for him. Or was it just half a sentence that slipped in as the Apostles' Creed slipped by me. Since that day, I have a richer sense of the presence of those who have gone before us, and who are present to me, in Christ, at this moment. I remember as a child running into the church at Killeen, saying Our Fathers and Hail Marys for the 'poor souls' in Purgatory. They were pretty real then. It took a visit to a little village and the benediction of an old man to bring them back to me. Now I think about them, I talk to them, pray to them and pray for them. I treasure that man's gift to me in a small village behind a muddy swamp in Sierra Leone.

The Italian-American volunteer, Anne Doyle, in a delightful unpublished memoir which she wrote after she left Sierra Leone writes:

"As I look back at my efforts to help the people of Sierra Leone my greatest joy was believing we could share the gift of service with one another. I believe that the greatest injustice inflicted on the poor is the assumption that they have little to give. I have been richly blessed by the poorest of the poor. Wealthy nations pour money into developing countries as if money is needed for happiness, health, and peace. It simply is not true". We both could say with Gibran, "For this I bless you most: You give much and know not that you give at all". Creative and vivacious, Anne thoroughly enjoyed the give-and-take of village life. She has become a very dear friend, one with whom one can laugh and bubble in the shallows and swim serenely in life's depths.

Things do not always work in the village. Kpetewoma is one of the larger section towns of Lugbu Chiefdom and lies along the basin of the Sewa river where gem diamonds are found. The town straggles along both sides of the river; houses of people native to the place would have zinc roofs and glass windows and some sanitation. The village was inundated with diamond prospectors in the dry season, when the river was low; they peppered the place with small shacks, without order or sanitation. Such people made no real contribution to the development of the town. Diamonds there excel in quality and quantity and are found alluvially. Just dig down a metre or three and you may be a millionaire. Or again you may not.

Diamonds in Sierra Leone are at once the country's greatest asset and one of its major problems. The lure of the 'fast buck' is as old as money and as universal as people. Diamonds filter out of the country in various ways and do little for the national economy. Predictably, the Government has many laws governing the digging and sale of diamonds but places are remote, the forest is dense, and who is going to see? Talking about health in a place like that was like talking to the moon. Could we not see they would argue that if a man was lucky and got a big diamond, he would have money for medicines and all would be well. Never mind the deplorable sanitation, the overcrowding, and the high rates of communicable diseases. Just wait. When they got the big diamond . . . The difficulty of introducing self-reliant practices, or community action for preventive health care, in such a village, was enormous. Anne Doyle and Paul Harding were initiating village committee activities at the time. Anne writes:

"My efforts to organise a health committee in Kpetewoma never came to fruition. I believe there was a lesson of importance in my efforts there, and a gift received in the end. It was a diamond-mining town of some four thousand people with a wide range of tribes and varied economies. The traditional structure had become unsettled and I never felt sure where to address my queries. As in all six villages I had arranged an initial week of teaching, during which I would live in a room provided by that town. The Mende pride themselves on their hospitality to a stranger. It had been my experience that a Mende village was the true meaning of the word WELCOME."

When she arrived in Kpetewoma however, on the return visit, when they were to have chosen the members of the committee, she was met by no one. No one had been given responsibility for her feeding and, to add insult or injury, the town chief gave her two Leones, the equivalent of one dollar, to go and find food for herself and her companion. As there was no restaurant anyway this was hopeless. Nurse Paul, himself a Mende, was aggrieved and embarrassed. Other villages, he knew, would harvest a collective farm especially for visitors. She continues: "By the end of the third day the Chief was still asking who would feed us. The Health Committee they had nominated had not managed to meet as a group and my enthusiasm and patience had long since dwindled. I called a meeting of the elders and anyone else concerned, to share my feeling of frustration. Their only reply was to shake their heads and say 'Oh Kpetewoma!'".

Since it looked as if the town had slipped its traditional moorings and even the people themselves did not recognise this, she decided to throw in the towel. "I gave them what I could not easily part with – my anger, and they named me 'Gbandia'. The word means to warm up or to put fire under. It was bestowed on me during a confrontation of stern words that ended in laughter and I felt they understood me. We parted standing equally together each holding our separate dreams."

Anne went home when her contract was finished, but Primary Health Care and committees continued to progress. Perhaps peer pressure from successful health centres in the area and the memory of Gbandia had their influence. Eventually a delegation from Kpetewoma came to my office asking that I would visit their town. When I arrived, a large crowd had gathered to greet me. They all shook my hand, told me how young I was keeping and then led me proudly to the health centre site. They had already laid the foundation and I shared their sense of achievement. When the centre was completed it was staffed by the Ministry of Health and launched at a grand ceremony of food, wine and dancing. I often wondered if a large diamond had been found which had financed the project. Kpetewoma was not telling.

13

Rites of Passage

On a visit to a health centre in a nearby village I was told that there was a woman in labour and asked if I would come and see her. I was conducted to an enclosure behind a house where a young girl of no more than sixteen years of age was rebelling against the pains of labour and would not let anybody touch her. The older women have their own ways of dealing with this and not always very gentle ones. But now they were smiling the 'she will learn' smile. She reminded me of a deer – frightened, beautiful.

With a little coaxing she agreed to let me examine her. Soap and water were procured and I knelt by her side on the ground and found that she needed an assisted delivery that could be provided at the local hospital.

Traditionally a long labour has ominous implications for the woman. Believing it to be caused by marital infidelity, the attending women can coerce the patient into a 'confession' of the name of the lover. This is another example of who caused it, not what. Between this and conventional theories of causality there are often sharp conflicts. Of course I am unable to tell myself or anyone else why one woman's pelvis is small and another's is big; why one labour is long and another short; but I am certain, and so are the local people, that a confession does not affect favourably the birth of the baby. The confession however seems to have socio-religious significance above its immediate practical value.

In any case, I just said as boldly as I could: "I'm taking her to hospital". Normally these decisions involve senior family members, on both sides of the marriage if possible. Primary amongst them is, of course, the husband. Discussion at a time like this can be tragic for the patient if it takes 24 hours and the patient is in need of immediate surgery.

My announcement was received with apparent relief and quickly, as if it was a change of scene on stage, clothes were put on, a woman delegated to accompany her and off we went. She had a baby girl.

The birth of a child is a great event. Whenever I deliver a baby I am happy for the whole day. Babies are born, for the most part, at home in the village. The attending women greet the event with the greatest delight but they are also celebrating that a woman has come through a dangerous experience. Maternal mortality in Sierra Leone is 800 per 100,000 live births, making the risk of death in childbirth many times higher for a woman in the third world than for her sisters in the west.

During the nine months of the pregnancy a vast network of traditions and taboos surrounds the behaviour of the mother-to-be. If she has a 'pica' or longing for certain foods she should be given them or the baby may have large spots on the skin; she should not drink from a bottle or the baby will have an umbilical hernia; if she eats the larva of the giant beetle – reputed to be very delicious – the baby will have a segmented neck; if she eats okra, which is a slimy vegetable, she will have an easy birth, the okra being held to have lubricating properties; she should not eat sesame seed or the baby will be too talkative and so on.

Unfortunately, there is no advice about overwork so she weeds the rice farm during the rainy season, plants the vegetables she is going to use in her sauces, helps with harvesting of the rice which is done with a short knife in the right hand, the left hand grasping the stalks a hands breadth from the grain. She threshes it, parboils and stores it and eventually brings it to the table. In between she washes clothes, cooks meals, dries coffee beans, cracks palm kernel, spins cotton, harvests all other food and stores fish and other perishables without refrigerators. She it is who cares for the sick – the unending sickness of her children and the old people. If she is lucky she will already have a toddler on her back, so 'one on the back and one in the belly' makes her the valiant woman of her tribe.

She faces the high mortality of child-birth with equanimity. If it happens, it happens. Women living in these types of economies have learned to manage their grief, and live on. When the baby arrives all these dangers are forgotten. The women relatives will hold the baby with reverence and awe, as if it were the first baby they have ever seen, each one in turn exclaiming the soft, wondering 'Oh yah' of the Mende.

When the young mother in this story came home she did not leave the house again till the eighth day, which is, among other things, naming day. She was advised in the hospital to give the colostrum to the baby. This was not traditional. Granny was accustomed to give a little yam mashed to a pap, moistened with palm oil and placed on the baby's lips with the Granny's little finger. It is called the pap of life. The baby was not too interested in it so it hardly did her any harm

As the child was formally brought through the door she was taken in the arms of some revered member of the family and carried around the house. Who she is, what family she belongs to, what good things she must do in her life, what evil she must avoid, and what name she is to bear, was whispered meanwhile into her ear. A plate of food, with some cola nuts and some coins at the side of the plate, was placed at the mother's feet, wishing her and her child good luck.

The loveliest practice of all had taken place some days earlier when the umbilical cord dropped off. Granny took it and planted it together with a mango tree, the custom being to plant it with a food-bearing tree like coco-nut, guava, avocado, mango or citrus. The child will learn which is her tree and will visit it throughout life, on returning to the place of her birth. It is not surprising that trees feature very prominently in Mende tradition.

I looked at this little mite and recalled my mother once telling me that, when I was first handed to her, she looked at me and said: "I wonder what is before you, a ghrá". I wondered and prayed for this child. Little more than a quarter of live births reach their fifth birthday. Having encouraged the mother to attend clinic and avail of all the child's immunisations, I wished baby Hilary (didn't I say it was naming day?) and her mother all the blessings in the world and left them to the joy of this new life.

A Funeral: The mother of the driver at the hospital had died. She was an old lady, her son Mustapha being already a grandfather. But he said she was not old. She came from a village in Pujehun District where the war had already started and the village was too near the rebel lines for safety. She had only just reached her son in Bo when one of the gastro-intestinal diseases claimed her and she died.

The family is Muslim. She must therefore be buried on the same day she dies. It was necessary to get a van to take the corpse and some mourners to the village that, as I have said, was very near rebel lines. Vehicles in Bo Town were not anxious to go there. But as the late woman was a senior member of the local Chapter of the women's society, it was of paramount importance that her grave would be located in her village.

Sister Anita in the development office provided a van and I had a jeep. We went to the local military post, asked for a safe pass with our sad little cortege and arrived in the village without mishap. The women had not heard of the death and our arrival with her corpse was the occasion of the traditional wailing. Wailing is sudden, spreads like a bush fire and amplifies in a grand crescendo filling the village with its sound. The traditional crying at Irish wakes did not, as far as I know, start immediately the death occurred. It was called 'keening' and was used to recount the excellence of the deceased. In Sierra Leone its suddenness and volume is startling.

I found myself sitting in the barri, while they got ready for the funeral, thinking of the day it was, Holy Thursday. For us Christians it is the memorial of the last supper of Jesus before his execution, and his message of love and unity. No one here was Christian, and I thought back to Killeshandra on Holy Thursday: the extravaganza of flowers on the altar of repose, the sweet heady scent of St. Joseph's lilies as we tried to stay awake during adoration. Did I ever think that, one day, I would spend the day so far away liturgically.

When the wailing had subsided, the women left the barri where the men had gathered and in a little while they returned. They burst in from between some houses, singing and dancing, strong and coherent. They reached the men and as many as possible were seated. The chosen spokeswoman was young, perhaps mid forties, a fine looking woman, confident, without being aggressive, and well briefed. She started to speak. She said that the women had lost a leader, a leader whose subordinate groups stretched over the whole section of the chiefdom. They were asking, she said, for two young girls to be assigned to them for initiation into the society, along with a goat, a bushel of rice, a four gallon tin of palm oil, four thousand Leones and a head-scarf.

The men were asking for some reduction in the demands. Their demand was rejected. This lady could negotiate. I was familiar with all these requests: the girls represented the continuity of the society; the rice, oil and a warm-blooded animal signified the sustaining of life. These I was familiar with, but I did not know the meaning of the headscarf. Society elders do wear a white one. Now there was more discussion and money was being collected and passed on to Mustapha, the son of the deceased. It was touched to the earth before he took it in his hand and put it away. This sense of belonging to the created world, of environmental interdependence is powerful and ritually honoured in many similar ways. Some traditions tell us, that the introduction of shoes was not welcome because of losing contact with the earth, a thought that finds an echo in Hopkins' line: "nor can foot feel being shod".

I did not stay for the actual burial. They had started digging the grave there in the village – not the greatest public health practice. I knew that the coffin used was for transporting only and that the body, wrapped in white cotton sheeting, would be slipped gently into the grave without it. I knew too that a country cloth, which is hand woven in local cotton and very special, would be draped on the coffin and, just before the burial, the youngest child of the deceased, would catch up a corner of the cloth, and then run with it as far away as possible *without looking back*. The latter is very important. To look back may reveal the deceased sitting on the grave. One explanation I have been given for this is that the youngest child is the most beloved of the parent who may want to take the child with them.

Another interesting custom at funerals is that the family address the deceased, giving messages for loved ones gone before or bidding the deceased farewell. Once I stood at a graveside of a young boy of twelve who had been killed in a senseless road traffic accident. I watched the young body go down into the rich, beautiful earth, to mingle with the earth's substance and commence interaction with water, plants, solar and stellar systems, with the entire cosmos. The father spoke: "Good-bye now," he said, "Forgive us for the times we were hard on you. We meant well. Pray for us and pray for the country".

A Marriage: Kadie was twenty and a widow with one child. She had not been to school but was initiated into her tribe, and had become a promising young member of her society. She worked at the hospital as a cook, had become a Catholic and knew that church marriage was expected of her. One day she told me that she had a prospective husband and would like to marry in church. She asked for my support in approaching her family with Dauda, the prospective groom. I was quite willing but took advice from seniors of the clan and we made an appointment to go to Kadie's village some sixteen miles away.

When we arrived there we were met by the family members. A sizable crowd gathered to see the nature of this extraordinary expedition, composed as it was of several important looking men, and one white woman. Once our greetings had been exchanged, the families dismissed the extras, saying "we have business". We then proceeded into the house where the elders of Kadie's family, men and women, were assembled. Our leader then got up and gave the head of the household some coins, amounting to about two pounds. He accepted the money, looked around at the other members of the family and displayed the money. He then addressed the leader: "why have you given us this money?" Negotiations thus formally opened, the leader introduced the nature of our business. Dauda was introduced and more greetings followed. At this point the head of the family addressed Dauda and asked him where he came from and what family he belonged to. The latter seemed to be very important. Fortunately for Dauda he was able to name a well-known person to whose family he was connected. The family exchanged satisfied glances. Because of the formality of the proceedings I had begun to feel a little tense; I wondered if our quest would go through smoothly but now I began to feel better. The next question was: " where have you been since you grew to manhood?" He disclosed that he had been in Freetown and Bo learning to be a tailor. Then he played his trump card: he had his own sewing machine. Everything was now becoming more positive and the men of the family rose to shake Dauda's hand once more. The women had said nothing so far.

The speaker for the family then said: "We de go hang head", meaning they would put their heads together; the men got up and went out one door and the women and Kadie went out the other. Since Kadie had chosen this man herself I felt happy that there was no element of coercion. The subject of the dowry, which the groom must pay, was introduced very delicately. After much haggling between the delegation and the family we agreed on fifteen pounds to be paid to Kadie's family by Dauda. After this had been handed over the women pointed out that there was no 'cold water' for them in the arrangement. I had discovered long before that 'cold water' meant refreshments, soft drinks and, of course, palm wine. Another couple of pounds were handed over.

The next item on the agenda surprised me. The family expressed their sincere gratitude for the caring for their children shown by our coming to see them and spending time with them. As a mark of their esteem they invited us to be involved in the on-going support of these two young people and, binding us to this, shared one pound of the dowry with each one of us. In accepting the money we pledged ourselves to this trust. I received this pound in my hand and was deeply moved at my inclusion in this family's life circle. Dauda and Kadie were married in the church in Serabu in a very quiet and unobtrusive ceremony. They had explained that their station in life did not demand wedding expenses such as they had observed in other Christian weddings. Common sense like that augured well for them and indeed they raised a fine family and gave none of us any reason to honour the pound other than keeping in touch with them and their children.

14

Brave Heart

Almost every house has a barri. Some call it a palaver hut but it is more of an outside parlour, a place to relax, to meet people. It is an ideal place to entertain people, or interview the numerous people who come for one thing or another. Most of these structures have a hammock but not ours. The main problem with our barri was its location. It was situated in such a way that by the time one reached it one was already on the way out, usually in a hurry.

Jeremiah was a regular customer at the barri. 'Grumpy' was the only word that came to mind for him. He always complained about his life, his fate, and his present lack of funds, and on and on. Added to that he had the misfortune to arrive at our barri at a moment when I am on my way somewhere else, thus bringing frustration and compassion into sharp conflict. I find this an uncomfortable emotional mix to start the day with.

Jeremiah has little reason to rejoice and cannot easily figure out the best time to come. He is totally blind. One day I asked him to come on Saturday morning when I was free and we would sit down and have a chat.

This is what he told me. As a young man he decided to become a tailor. This is a reasonably lucrative job in Sierra Leone. A sewing machine is a staff of life. He did a three-year apprenticeship and was about to set up his own tailoring shop when he had a dream. He dreamed that someone came and dropped something in each of his eyes and the next day his eyes started to give trouble. He went to see Dr Gess, a Methodist Missionary ophthalmologist in Bo; a man as saintly as he was skilled in his profession. According to Jeremiah, Dr Gess said he would operate on his eyes and gave him a date for surgery. But the night before he was due for surgery he had another dream. A very black 'devil' came and sat on his chest and pressed very hard. Next day Dr. Gess pronounced him inoperable.

That is the story as Jeremiah perceived it. He was uncertain about the time frame for all those happenings, but eventually he became completely blind.

Herbal medicine is usually tried in these circumstances and indeed Jeremiah verified that his family sought this measure. The one he remembers was that herbs were collected in the bush, boiled and a mixture prepared. He was asked to put his face into this fluid with his eyes open. It stung bitterly, he said, as if it were pepper.

I asked whether he or his family 'bin luk gron'. This is a Krio expression that derives from the English to "look at the ground" and is a metaphor used to seek the underlying cause. Jeremiah said the 'luk gron' did yield information that some 'bad people' were involved – unspecified. And anyway he said, he was blind by that time and what was to be done? "How for do?" he said, "Whateva God mark, so i go be", meaning: "there is nothing to be done; what ever God decides will come to pass." "For bear". Just put up with it. Even Jeremiah's deity was an oppressor.

Traditional management of ophthalmic conditions is less than scientific and I have seen much destruction wrought by over vigorous application of herbal and other remedies.

I have often wondered whether there was, in the first dream, a pointer to some reality and that he feared to face, and whether he then responded with an abrasive medicine? Who knows? Right now he has complete opacity of both cornea with a leash of blood vessels converging centrally. Short of a bi-lateral corneal transplant, Jeremiah will never see again.

Jeremiah was directed to a local school for the blind where he learned to make doormats from local materials procured from the bush. This had its own difficulties because he had to find someone to fetch them, and in the monsoon this was not feasible. He makes good mats. The material is strong raffia and the first three fingers on each hand are bulbous from the work.

But the market for mats is limited. They last long and not everyone buys them. Most convents and missions have mats at every door and even places where there is no door.

He is led about by a little boy who, he says, is his nephew, the child's mother having died. He tries to pay the boy's school fees and just now he needs a little help for the uniform. We can assist him over his bad patches because other people assist us over ours.

After that interview I watched him leave the compound and wondered what it would be like to walk about in a dark world led by a little child. And I renamed him Brave Heart.

Saint Francis Was Not Poor: One day Alimamy came. He was a tall, lanky Limba tribes man, from a minority group in the north of the country. They are widely noted for wine tapping. He wanted a job. Asked what skills he had he said he would do anything. This 'anything' nearly always means that the person has no particular skills but is desperate to work. And indeed he was desperate having a wife and two very small children, no job and no resources. We took Alimamy on as an odd jobs man and he turned out to be a good worker, competent and obliging, though a little given to reverie and talking to himself. The latter he claimed was his way of 'blowing out his mind' when angry about something he could do nothing about. Catching him one day in the kitchen with his hand on the tap, in one of his reveries, looking away into the distance over the bamboo trees, I offered him the proverbial penny for his thoughts. "I am thinking about my life", he said, and he began to unroll it.

He was born into a family where his father, his two wives and seven children owned a small groundnut farm. Alimamy could see little future for him on that small farm. So one day he told his mother that he was leaving and would go to the capital, find employment and would be 'sending' for her, which meant the occasional present or money.

"What did she say?"

"She said nothing only turned her face away."

Mama knew too much about the promises from the big city.

He boarded a 'poda poda' – a small pickup – bound for Freetown where he joined the multitude of the unemployed. Eventually a relative procured him a job loading trucks in a biscuit factory. There in the sweltering heat, humidity and dust he bent his long back, heaving large boxes on to a truck till the cool of the evening when he went to his lodgings. His kinsmen found him a corner in an already overcrowded house. Most of the houses in the Freetown slums, as in all city slums, are a health hazard; they are badly ventilated, sanitation is poor or non existent; bedbugs, mosquitos, and rats are common infestations. With his hand straying to his stomach Alimamy said: "at least there was something to eat which is the main thing"

Then his father died and he returned to the village. At a family gathering it was decided that he would farm their groundnut farm with his elder brother. Soon afterwards, however, the brother died of a snakebite. Alimamy did not inherit the farm in the subsequent family shake up. This time he headed south where the River Sewa flowed over and through a bed of gem diamonds. Or so the story goes. Every young man's Eldorado. Again he explained this move by his right hand reaching the seat of survival, his stomach.

Such young men are hired by 'big men' – important, wealthy men. They stand ankle or knee deep in the swamp all day washing gravel and looking for gems, which they are supposed to give up to their master. Sometimes they steal the gems, but since they are not licensed dealers they are obliged to sell to a middleman for a pittance. More often they are caught and are fired or imprisoned. To make a long story longer, all Alimamy got out of that was a troublesome cough and, wonder of wonders, a wife.

"How come you had the courage to marry without money, job, family, or prospects?" I asked, and while I said it I thought back to Ireland in the twenties and thirties where people had the same kind of courage. He kept his hand on the tap, all the while letting the precious water run – a crime in the dry season – but I did not dare to stop him, so lost in his life's journey was Alimamy. He did not look my way, but explained that she was the foster child of a woman he was lodging with and this woman liked him and offered him the girl. The girl also liked him. He said he had no money for the dowry but the foster-mother said that that could wait and he took the girl to wife. "You see", he continued, "if a man has a few children he may have something", and he waved his hand nebulously in the air, "to put in his stomach in the end". Again the hand came to rest on the stomach. But even the marriage started a long train of troubles. The woman who gave him the wife was not the natural parent and strictly speaking had not the giving of her. Now, two children later, both parties are pressing for some marriage money. We helped him with his problem.

'Something for the stomach' seemed to be the length, breadth and depth of Alimamy's ambition. Obtaining a job with the sisters, two rent-free rooms for him and his wife and children, wages, food to eat and free medical treatment was his first real break through. When we found that his cough was indeed what we suspected it to be, tuberculosis, we set up his treatment and kept him on. What else could we do? He must have something in the stomach.

He idolised his two small daughters, his love and his social security, but he loved Damsey 'pass all'. At two years old she jumped and frolicked around, following her dad to work. They sang songs together, and had great discussions. At five she had a uniform and went to primary school. He was so proud of her. Illiterate himself, he dreamt of education for his children at all costs and saved up a few Leones monthly. I kept them for him and matched them one for one. Mary, the younger, was a slow developer and did not walk till she was eighteen months old. This left her very dependent on her mother. Damsey proclaimed to us all one day that she was her father's child and Mary belonged to her mother.

"Mama" she explained "borned Mary, but Papa borned me"

When the war came near he fled with his wife and two little girls to a safe place. To our horror and his, the fighting erupted right near where he had placed them. Desperate, he raced back looking for them but was barred access to the area by the military. Then the fighting broke out in another area as it kept on doing and Alimamy tried again and found them. All the family were together again but only for a few months, until the Sisters were all evacuated because of the war. And now I think of Alimamy and his lovely daughters and plucky little wife and I wonder what has become of his dreams, as he struggles for 'something to put in the stomach' for the four of them. It was Patrick Kavanagh who has said that St. Francis was not poor, because he had a choice. The poor have no choices.

I will not let Alimamy's dreams die, if I can locate him. If his children are alive I shall somehow manage to send school fees to them because dreams are infectious and his have become mine.

Rogues in the System: It would be nice if I could record that on all days and at all times I have personally received all comers with the grace and courtesy of Christ, which I planned in the morning. What becomes of these plans? Sometimes when I'm just sitting down to a meal, or to write a letter, and I am tired and the day long, and I am called, I would say: "I wish the poor and needy were poor and needy somewhere else!" If such visitors were sick then the morning's resolutions would take over swiftly. This, however, was not always the case. An example was George, whom I encountered in

Cameroon where I spent three years after being displaced from Sierra Leone. He was homeless and had been found sleeping in the street and either begging or stealing for his living. Fr. Brian Byrne of St. Patrick's Missionary Society, teaching in a local secondary school, had taken up the cause of the homeless in his spare time. Accommodation and one good meal a day had been provided for George but the call of the street was strong. Invariably he got into trouble and would need minor health adjustments by the time he was rescued. He was amiable and pleasant and displayed those qualities with a wide smile, half fatuous and entirely friendly. When George presented himself at the convent I would admonish him for not going directly to the hospital. But George always had some trump up his sleeve. This time it was a letter:

Dear Hilary,
   'Enclosed' is George . . .
   A special gift to you
   As he has been
   To many Missionaries
   Over many Missionary years
   Until love and patience
   Thought to be immeasurable
   Both drained away
   But I'll ask you to have him
   Only for a week or two
   As it is Passiontide
   And he'll be the image
   For this period
   Of the station
   I forget the number
   Where a woman
   Wiped the Sacred Face
   Of the suffering Jesus
   And this is George

This Passiontide
With the mischievous
Twinkle in his eye
And truly it can be
More than mischievous . . .
But see a smile of love
A Jesus smile
An Easter smile
For you.   Brian Byrne S.P.S.

There was also Christopher who had more serious health problems than George and needed hospital care from time to time. He also would gain admission to hospital on the strength of a magic letter from a mutual friend. Unlike George, who would break your heart and steal a piece of it, whose smile was wide, explained all things, and tripped you up in the middle of the sentence you had ready to deal with him, Christopher was serious, demanding and rather truculent. He would come to my office to convince me, at length, that he knew better ways of solving some problems than I did, if only I would listen to him. Amongst his priorities was the condition of the toilets; these, he claimed, could be kept in very good order if I had them locked up. To demonstrate the efficacy of this method he locked up all the toilets one night, leaving a female patient imprisoned in one of them.

Understandably the nursing staff had little welcome for this category of patient and even less for prisoners. In Cameroon the prisoners who came to see us were almost always those awaiting trial, a situation they often had to endure for months or even years. When discharged from the hospital they went back to prison where the conditions were deplorable. If they picked up a little of the hospital or another patient's property on the way one could hardly blame them. Sometimes they escaped. One way or another they made endless problems for the nurses, who sometimes scolded, but in the end, always accepted and loved them.

Sometimes you start for the Barri with suppressed irritation, to meet an unwelcome visitor at an awkward time of day. This can be a humbling experience, when you discover instead someone who has come with a gift of a few bananas, oranges or a papaya. My elderly neighbour, who regularly brought luscious papayas, required, as a matter of great importance, that the old plastic bag he brought the fruit in, be returned to him. As I hand it to him I experience a moment of amazement that there are places in this high tech world where a plastic bag is property.

Yesterday, Today and Tomorrow: There is a horticulture unit attached to the Ministry of Agriculture in Bo. At one time it was flourishing and young people were trained to prune and plant, to nurse and name the beautiful shrubs, trees, and flowers of Sierra Leone.

Time has passed. As the economy failed horticulture drifted down to the bottom of the priority pile. Sadly, in most places it is now a relic of former times, attracting very little of the budget.

But what one does find is old people, old gardeners, who must have been beautifully trained in their day. One is Pa Momoh. I wonder what age he is. He looks in his seventies. His body is small and frail, as old people often are. He has early Parkinson's disease and toddles along, head first, and has a fairly coarse tremor in the hand that holds the secateurs. His clothes are old, at least those he wears in the garden, and since they belong to a former era of body substance, keeping the trousers up is a problem. He always has a pipe in his mouth, while his right hand holds a secateurs, so that between the pipe, the secateurs and holding up the trousers one would expect him to be uncoordinated but indeed he is not. He is always busy but never hurried. The pipe is not always lit and sometimes it is upside down.

One day, as he came to our garden, the place looked to me drab and overgrown. Our efforts at gardening were hampered by the fact that water is at a premium in the dry season, nor were they helped by the termites that ate up most things that we planted. In moving without speed or apparent excitement, Pa seemed as if he had entered a room where all there were familiars. "Ah," he said, "Plumbago Capensis. There is none in the whole of Bo right now. We used to have it in Njala". Moving on he greeted 'Lagarstroemia Indica', 'Gardenia Augusta', and when I pointed out 'Yesterday, Today, and Tomorrow', he gently corrected me: "But we would call it Brunfelsia Uniflora . . ." Brunfelsia has much the same fragrance as gardenia, but the difference is that gardenia comes in white and goes in white, whereas this one has blooms in three colours at any time of the day, some blue, some white and some purple. Pa now found a very old friend and he stood looking up at our straggling, untidy Blushing Hibiscus. This plant is called botanically 'Hibiscus Mutabile'. It is truly one of the wonders of a tropical garden. The plant itself is straggly, its branches growing in disorderly fashion in every direction like uncombed hair. The bloom of this unlikely shrub comes in large flowers like peony roses only bigger. They are snow white in the morning, and turn gradually through a delicate pink to a deep red as the day wears on. At night it folds up looking like a red, red rose, beautiful even in death. For a party, one can put them in the fridge in the morning and take them out in the evening and they will go through their change performance in the course of the evening. Pa gazed at it and murmured: "White in the morning, pink at noon and red in the evening – changes of life". Turning to me, he said: "If you want to know how God works, look at that".

He went on with his shuffling forward kind of toddle, always busy but never hurried, preparing cuttings for planting, remembering some English man with whom he worked in the long ago times and merging with the plants and the earth.

While he was there I had a sense of timelessness and peace.

Closing on the Hens: In the small town of Danballa, twelve miles from Bo one Sunday evening at 6:45 p.m., my friend Sr. Teresa McKeown of the St Joseph of Cluny Sisters went to put in her free-range chickens. They were a little frolicsome so she chased them happily. Suddenly, she disappeared down an empty well. This prospective water-well had been dug in the preceding dry season and, as it was unpromising, was abandoned and covered with a piece of wood. During the rainy season the wood had rotted. Teresa stepped on it and down she went. It was between fifteen and twenty feet deep.

Finding herself alive and fairly intact, she took stock of her situation and her co-habitants. There was a little water, a lot of leaves and some living things rustling around, probably as shocked as herself at her unceremonious arrival. Quickly she spotted the snake and as quickly stepped on it. Preliminaries over, she began to shout.

Her location was some three hundred yards from the house, and to complicate matters, the only other people in the house that weekend were two guests. Not being familiar with the house routine, they did not miss her for some time and, when they did, it was already dark. There were very few places she could be. Nearest house? No. She was not there. Then began the search in earnest.

Meanwhile, back in the well, Teresa watched the evening light fade and the stars come out in the small circle of world above her. Then the generator came on and with it the first stirrings of panic. Could she stay here all night? What else was scudding around her feet? Was that snake really dead? The Irish believe themselves to hold a charm from St. Patrick against snakes, but alone with a snake in a well, what comfort was that? It was not an article of faith.

However, Teresa did have faith, but not charms. She did her relaxation exercises. She spoke with the Lord about her predicament. She spoke with the spirits of her parents and family deceased. They felt near. She spoke with the ancestral spirits of the chiefs and people of the village who had given the land she was living on, and she touched lovingly the walls of her surroundings, keeping in touch with reality. So engaged, she did not feel faint until a storm lantern shone dimly above her and the awed voice of a villager said, "Lawd 'ave me'cy!" Awash with relief, the first feeling of faintness appeared, but now people were talking above her and she stood firm.

It took a lot longer to haul her up than it did for her to go down. By the time I arrived she was in bed. My delight on finding that she had no back injury quite limited my sympathy for some possible injury to a small bone in one foot, and indeed miraculously, beyond shock and some bruises she only had one small bone fracture in the foot. She had been wearing a very good brand of shoes. Come to think of it she should do a 'promo' for them.

Sir Milton Magai first Prime Minister of Independent Sierra Leone

Paramount Chief Makavore of Serabu. During his internment in Freetown, for his activities in the hut-tax war (1898), he met and invited the Catholic Mission to Serabu. The Mission opened in 1904

Family group in The Colony: Father and a relative standing in the doorway. Mother, seated, holds me on her right, Betty on her lap and Josie in the chair

The Clapper Bridge built about 1850 holds many happy childhood memories

Kneeling with Sr. Lucy (R) at the altar having just received
the habit and a new name

In front of the Secret Society house, Mama Kema and her grand children
welcome me to their village

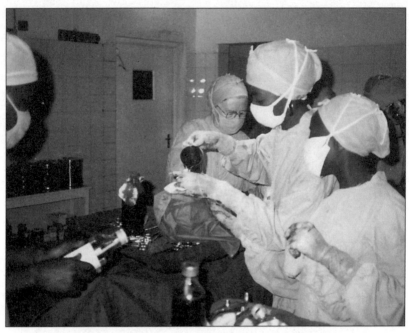

Scooping up blood from the abdomen with a small jug, filling ACD bottles
and infusing the blood immediately saved many lives

The Barri. Cool and shaded it served as an outside parlour in which
to relax, discuss or entertain

Serabu Convent built by Fathers Joe Jackson and Harold Heard in 1948

The Convent was destroyed during the war in 1995

The Children's ward at Serabu built with help from Misereor,
Caritas and Oxfam in 1969

All the Hospital buildings including the Children's ward were destroyed
during the war 1995

15

The Remains of the Day

Looking back: my life in Sierra Leone was a good life, and I enjoyed it. I thoroughly enjoyed village ways and, later, enjoyed national health planning with medical colleagues in Freetown. There was a time when I wanted to immerse myself in African culture and even considered taking out Sierra Leone nationality. I was disabused on that score by a beggar in Freetown who asked me what nation I belonged to. When I lightly answered, "Mende" he shot back: "Fodon nar wata no turn fish", – what falls into the water does not become a fish. I gradually came to realise that I relate best to people by being myself. And I am Irish – Irish as the bogs and meadows of Mayo.

Memory tends to distil from life the happy times but memory must be honest as it seeks out the shadows.

Africa grew up into changing mores, life styles and educational status and this was inevitable, and, to a large extent, welcome. Yet anxiety and fear began to haunt us as the economy declined and an ever-widening chasm developed between the rich and the poor. The cause now was a witch called 'Greed' that lay deep in the hearts of the few who cared nothing for the plight of the many.

A young church grew up as I grew old. The clergy, now indigenised and educated, began to take their measure of the missionaries. We had brought the faith, they said, already inculturated in the culture of our origins with little esteem for the indigenous faith, vision and traditions of the people we had come to evangelise. These allegations, appearing in various 'mission media' were, at first bewildering but in retrospect were partially, at least, justified. Missiology, how to approach the people's own 'supernatural', was not a feature of our training, though our founder Bishop Shanahan was aware of its importance.

Changes in the practices of religious life were traumatic for some. Since those changes were intertwined with all the other changes taking place around us, in the church, in society and in the health field, it sometimes felt that we were standing on shifting sand. We can now laugh retrospectively at such preoccupations as whether or not to wear a veil: big worries about small issues. An underlying fear that our lives were falling apart was unspoken but operative. Many, in fact, left the Holy Rosary and other congregations.

For a number of years, Holy Rosary Sisters had, where possible, handed over the management of institutions to indigenous personnel and taken subordinate positions. 'Working ourselves out of a job' had always been a focussed policy. Now that it seemed we had succeeded there was a feeling that a particular missionary era was over and with great poignancy I recalled Peg Sayer's words on leaving the Blaskets as appropriate to our situation: "People will yet walk above our heads, it can even happen that they will walk into the graveyard where I'll be lying but *people like us will never again be there*. (Italics mine). We'll be stretched out quietly – and the old order will have vanished."

Retrospectively I can recollect moments of loneliness when I missed Ireland and its lovely four seasons. I missed my family and was especially sad not being home when my parents died; obviously I missed opportunities for self-development in my own culture in fields of art, drama, literature, history and the ever-evolving socio-political scenes. But that is looking back. In Africa I was happy.

And then came the war. A crippling, meaningless, purposeless war broke out and the unthinkable happened. It started in the December of 1990 on the Sierra Leone/Liberian border. We just considered it a fracas between border soldiers over loot. It soon spread. A coup followed. The fighting continued. Marauding groups made flash appearances in villages, perpetrating the atrocities we have become familiar with – decapitation, disembowelling, limb amputation, rape and looting. There was a massive refugee exodus to Guinea where some of our sisters went to serve and have remained.

Beryl Markam, in her book *West With the Night* writes: " I have learned that if you must leave a place that you have lived in and loved and where your yesterdays are buried deep – leave it in any way except a slow way, leave it in the fastest way you can".

We left fast. In January 1995, as seven sisters were taken hostage by the fighting men and the country's most productive and most heavily guarded mines were attacked, we decided to leave. We who felt we had done so much could now do nothing. Numb with grief I packed two suitcases, occupied myself with much busy-ness as I had done leaving The Colony long ago, and walked away from a lifetime.

This was so unlike our Founder's experience. When leaving Nigeria for health reasons in 1930, he wrote to one of our sisters:

"While I write I can see you still as you all stand on the burning red clay of Nigeria while we moved away over the cool waters on our way to exile in so-called comfort in Ireland – Ireland now become a place of exile for African missionaries."

I did not feel as Bishop Shanahan did. All I remember about my leaving was the many and varied business affairs that had to be attended to: packing, locking, looking for safe keeping for the car, paying salaries and wages, saying good-bye to the few friends that were around and making arrangements for travelling. My feelings were packed away, like my clothes, in some emotional suitcase, to be opened at a future date. Later I read an entry in my journal while in Cameroon. It is headed: "Talking to myself" and it reads: "I am happy in Cameroon. Of course. Then why have I left the evening prayer in chapel and why am I standing out here by myself watching the setting sun and wondering if it is leaving a golden streak on the Atlantic in Freetown and now why are tears streaming down my face"? There is an African proverb that says "return to old watering holes for more than water – friends and dreams are there to meet you". My watering holes were not in Cameroon.

Returning to Ireland I watched as the fortunes of Sierra Leone waxed and waned. I heard that the hospital at Serabu had been destroyed and many villagers killed. Then in 1999 Freetown was attacked. For sheer savagery this attack beggars the English language to describe. I cringed in horror as TV footage showed arms and legs hacked off, decapitated bodies on the street, burned out buildings, women, children and men running for shelter or being beaten to death. The unimaginable had happened.

Back to the Beginning: For me the sense of loss was enormous. Forty-two years of my living were spent in Sierra Leone. I had identified more completely than I knew with the hopes and aspirations of that country. There I had lived mainly among a farming people who were hard working and easy going like country people anywhere. I felt the need to go back and see the place and meet the people once more. After an interval of five years in March 2000 I had that privilege.

My first stop was Freetown. At first sight it looked the same. Lots of colour, bright sunshine and great numbers of people in the streets, going about their business, created a sense of homecoming. Then a small boy was at the car asking for alms, holding up one of his stumps and suddenly you know that this was not the same country you had left. It was the same on meeting old friends. It felt like old times. Then came the stories of horrors seen and suffered like ghosts that will not rest. At the Ministry of Health I was told that ten thousand bodies were buried from the streets and shallow graves in January 1999. There also I learned that, understandably, all health personnel were engaged in emergency services demanded by the war. It will take a long time to re-plan and redirect health services into the more developmental aspects of Primary Health Care. Additionally reconciliation and rehabilitation will have to be the prevailing rural dynamic for years to come. This destruction of plans that were viable and that took years and human resources to set in motion is one of the hidden casualties of the war.

I spent a weekend in Bo where a great number of old friends came to meet me. We exchanged news of everyone. There were stories there too. Alimamy came running up the road looking more gaunt than I remembered him and slightly distraught. He told me that in the last run for safety his daughter Mary had died and he had not heard of his wife or his dear Damsey for over a year. He mentioned that his wife had been pregnant at the time of flight and then I felt for certain that she had died because she would have needed assisted delivery. In that case Damsey might have been lucky enough to be picked up by some good soul and survive. But among the thousands of such children identification will be almost impossible given the poor communications. "And how are you Alimamy and have you work?" I asked "I am digging diamonds" he said "Are you getting enough money?" "Enough to put something in the stomach" he answered, hand straying to the now very empty looking stomach. Alimamy is back where he started, the lights gone out.

I visited Serabu. Driving up through the village as I first did in 1954 felt like a homecoming. Quickly, however the difference manifested itself. Houses lay in ruins and some places I hardly recognised. Then I turned into the hospital compound as a thousand times before. First I went to the convent. Its blackened walls stuck up from the earth naked, without roof, windows or doors. I looked into the chapel but no vestige remained that would indicate its purpose. I was told it was torched while the women and children had taken refuge there, which left me numb with horror. The thought came to me that maybe growing things at least had survived, so I looked for the scarlet Bouganvillea that had rioted to the right of the front door, its branches dancing against the chapel window, but all that remained was a gnarled withered stick. With Ms Florence Bayo, Directress of the National Catholic Health Office, I walked around the hospital buildings. The roofs, windows, doors, equipment and furniture had been removed from every building except one small staff house. The bush reclaiming its old territory, was growing through any available crevice; it was with difficulty that I made my way into the operating theatre. But I succeeded and standing there prayed for everyone who had ever come through its doors. Back at the Community Health Office I looked for the lovely pink Hibiscus that grew there, but there was no sign of it. The disappearance of these things of beauty added to the sense of desolation. I took a last panoramic look at the ruined buildings. The jagged walls, thrusting through the bush, bear witness to a missionary era, to the energy, confidence and dedication of a small group of Holy Rosary Sisters over a span of forty-five years.

So what have I lost? Before the visit I felt washed up and lonely but in reality I have lost nothing because what has been is enshrined within me and remains forever part of me. I have lost nothing. When a senior nurse held my hand on parting and said: "We remember everything you taught us and are passing it on" I knew that life is about people and relationships. I recall with pride all the training I was involved in at village, district and national levels. They were good times full of hope and determination.

I will tell one final story of Serabu where my youth and dreams and excitements lie buried, where many of those I loved, fought with, laughed with, and cried with have their bones strewn in the grass and surrounding bush. Mr. Ahmadu Pessima whose services and friendship were so much a part of our early days had built a house near the hospital gate. It was not there when I returned. I asked about it and was told that the last of the family to live there was a daughter in law of Pa Pessima. A hard working woman all her life, she had a thriving vegetable garden and had stayed in Serabu during the rebel occupation. Her youngest son aged nineteen and a college student, advised her to leave, but she felt secure as she shared some produce with the rebels. He decided to stay with her. One day the rebels became convinced that her son was a spy for the Government. In vain did he protest his innocence. In front of her they drew their knives and said: "you will feel everything to the very end." He begged to be shot but they refused. His mother stumbled from the scene travelling many miles through the bush to safety.

I tell that story to celebrate the love and courage that brought that woman back to the scene. She found the remains of her son in the shreds of the pyjamas he had been wearing where they cut him down. She buried them with dignity and love. She lived a few more years in poor health and died trying to find forgiveness. With women like her, and there are very many, Sierra Leone will rise again even if, as Chesterton put it, the "night grows darker yet and the sea rises higher". Love is so much stronger than death and stronger than hatred. The darkness will not prevail.

I left Serabu in tears. They were not tears of despair, although that might have been natural. They were tears of solidarity with those who have suffered. I give thanks for that part of my life that I shared with them and am convinced, though I know not how or where, that we will meet again where all our tears will be wiped away.